Fr. Stan Fortuna, C.F.R.

Our Sunday Visitor Publishing Division
Our Sunday Visitor, Inc.
Huntington, Indiana 46750

Unless otherwise noted, the Scripture citations contained herein are from the *New Revised Standard Version Bible: Catholic Edition* (*The Catholic Youth Bible*) copyright © 1993, 1989 by the Division of Christian Education of the National Council of the Churches of Christ in the U.S.A. Used with permission. All rights reserved.

Excerpts from the English translation of the *Catechism of the Catholic Church, Second Edition*, for use in the United States of America, copyright © 1994 and 1997, United States Catholic Conference — Libreria Editrice Vaticana — are used with permission.

Quotations from the documents of the Second Vatican Council are taken from *The Documents of Vatican II*, Walter M. Abbott, S.J., General Editor, © 1966 by The America Press. Used with permission. All rights reserved.

Prayer to End Abortion, Prayer Before You Watch TV or Go to a Movie, Prayer Before You Go on a Date, Prayer After You Go on a Date, Prayer for Your Friends, Prayer for the Poor in the World, and Prayer for Self-Confidence are taken from *In the Zone — A Teen Guide to Prayer*, a resource developed by LIFE TEEN, Inc. Copyright © 2000 by LIFE TEEN, Inc. Used with permission. All rights reserved.

The quotations from the songs "Take My Heart" (from the CD *Take My Heart*); "Holy Masquerade" (from the CD *Loved By You*); "The Zipper Zone," "F.A.M.I.L.Y. (In-Laws)," and "Kumbya (Pass By My Way)" (from the CD *Sacro Song*); and "The Prayer of St. Augustine" (from the CD *First Collection*) are used with permission of Francesco Productions, 420 East 156th St., Bronx, NY 10465 (Website: www.francescoproductions.com). All rights reserved.

Every reasonable effort has been made to determine copyright holders and to secure permissions as needed. If any copyrighted materials have been inadvertently used without proper credit being given in one manner or another, please notify Our Sunday Visitor in writing so that future editions may be corrected accordingly.

Our Sunday Visitor Publishing Division
Our Sunday Visitor, Inc.
200 Noll Plaza
Huntington, IN 46750

ISBN: 0-87973-911-8
LCCCN: 2001-131196

Cover design and interior art by Tyler Ottinger
Interior design by Sherri L. Hoffman
Photos (cover and interior) by Mark Bowen/*The Catholic Telegraph*

PRINTED IN THE UNITED STATES OF AMERICA

Table of Contents

Preface

If you've ever looked at the hippopotamus in the zoo, or even in a photograph, you can easily conclude that God has a sense of humor, a great sense of humor. This creature is so awkward and so ugly that it could have been created only by Someone with a great sense of the ridiculous. In fact, the same is true of the giraffe and the blue-faced baboon. God loves them all, but they certainly show His sense of humor.

Our humorous God also plays practical jokes on us. He's done it with me. I love classical music — Bach and Puccini — as well as beautiful and refined English prose and poetry — Newman and Tennyson, Shakespeare and Francis Thompson. How did I ever get involved with "Gospel rap"?

It's a long story, but part of it is that years ago God sent Stan Fortuna — now Father Stan — into my life. Little did either one of us know that the Lord had special plans for us and our friends. When he was already in the seminary, I called Brother Stan one day and said to him, "The axe is laid to the root of the trees." That announced the beginning of the Franciscans of the Renewal.

The friars — and later the sisters — knew that we were called to follow St. Francis of Assisi in preaching by word and example a love for God (Father, Son, and Holy Spirit), for Christ (especially as He is present in the Holy Eucharist), for His holy mother, for the Church, and for the great bishop of the whole Church, Pope John Paul II. We knew we were sent especially to the poor and the homeless. The Lord made this clear to us through the powerful example of our dear and holy friend Mother Teresa of Calcutta. We now work with the poor, with their physical needs — often desperate needs — for food, clothing, shelter, and medical assistance. But we also preach

Christ and His Gospel to anyone who will listen, even a little bit — and the Holy Spirit does it all.

The friars began preaching frequently at Youth 2000 gatherings all over the world. Some — like me, for example — are not very good at it (I belong to "Youth 1950"). We also preach to cloistered nuns, to convicts, to charismatics and agnostics, to children, and even to intellectuals. The preaching in each case has to fit the message to the hearers. As St. Paul, who was so great at this, explained it: To the Jews he became a Jew, and to the Greeks a Greek (see 1 Corinthians 9:20-21).

Father Stan passionately believes that he is called to preach to a very hurt and cheated part of God's family — kids who have been raised on the media culture. He can speak its language, which I hardly comprehend. He can use its music, which I don't understand. He can see the problem from the inside, while I see only the outside and the bad results.

If you don't understand this strange land — the media world — don't judge Father Stan by what you like and don't like. In this book — which relies on the Bible, the *Catechism of the Catholic Church*, and the teachings of Pope John Paul II — Father Stan preaches the Gospel to a huge audience: young Christians who are the constant target of the spiritual and moral violence of the media, which I usually describe, when I'm trying to be kind, as a cesspool of toxic waste.

That Father Stan can do this is all the more remarkable since the Franciscans of the Renewal don't even have a television set, a computer, or, thank God, the Internet. By the way, we do have a pencil sharpener (manual).

This book is meant for kids who know and understand the media language. I wish they didn't. I wish it didn't exist. I think there should be a class action against everybody in MTV for corrupting the morals of minors. But I also wish that hurricanes didn't exist — but since they do, we have to face them. I wish that AIDS didn't exist, but we have to care for its victims and discourage its deadly contamination.

In every culture, good things survive because human nature, though wounded, is never totally depraved. This is the only reason the apostles could preach in Rome and Athens. This is why the faith survived the Nazis and the communists and their attempts to totally control and corrupt society.

I pray that *U Got 2 Believe!* will be a real help to many young men and women who want to follow Christ in this dark world, or who at least feel cheated by the culture in which we live. I hope that some will read this book who never read a religious book before. I ask the Holy Spirit to move them to open the Bible and the *Catechism of the Catholic Church*. I hope this book will help Father Stan in leading to Jesus Christ those who wouldn't listen to an old creature like myself.

(I even have a much less important personal hope, and that is that they may some day even listen to Bach, read Cardinal Newman, and learn to pronounce their words better and improve their spelling!)

FATHER BENEDICT GROESCHEL, C.F.R.
Feast of St. Clare
August 11, 2001

Foreword

How many of us have had billions of people talk about our lunch? What am I talking about?

Two thousand years ago there was a young man who went with his family to hear Jesus teach on the northern shores of the Sea of Galilee. Little did the boy know that the five loaves of bread and the two fish hidden in his backpack would in moments be the very focal point of the Son of God.

As the day began to draw to a close, the thousands who were listening to Jesus grew tired and hungry. The disciples' solution to this problem was to send the people away to get something to eat. But Jesus answered and said to them, "You give them something to eat!" Imagine being one of the disciples, and Jesus is looking you straight in the eye and asking you to do something that is obviously impossible. What do you do?

Well, the disciples did what most of us would do — they looked to their own strength. They replied, "Shall we go and spend two hundred days' wages on bread and give them something to eat?"

Jesus then forces His followers to take inventory of themselves by asking, "How many loaves do you have? Go look!" This is where that little boy's lunch, tucked away in his backpack, comes into play. The disciples asked the young boy if they could use the lunch for Jesus' purposes. The youngster was no doubt thrilled that in some small way Jesus could use something of his.

Jesus no doubt shocked the disciples when He acted as though five loaves and two fish would be enough to feed the crowd. He took the bread and fish, blessed them, and then broke the bread and gave back to the disciples even less than what they had started with.

Then came the moment of decision. Would the disciples face the crowd in obedience to Jesus, believing that Jesus could solve the problem using the little that they had in their hands; or would they hang their heads in silence, refusing to believe?

In order to turn around and face the crowd, U got 2 believe! And that is exactly what the disciples did. They fed a couple of people with the little they had in hand. But the question is, what do you do when you run out of bread and fish?

You go back to Jesus who is standing there with more bread and fish. Then you go out to the third and fourth hungry person, and then back to Jesus. Then to the fifth and sixth person, and then back to Jesus. The amazing thing about this demonstration of Jesus' power is that the entire crowd — five thousand men plus women and children — was fed, and that there was even food left over! How did this happen? One young boy gave Jesus the little he had, and that little was enough to change the world.

The key in this story is: What you have, in the hands of Jesus, is enough. What are your five loaves and two fish? What can you give to Jesus?

Start with your life! Then give Him every talent, every ability you have, no matter how small and insignificant you think it is. Then Jesus will do with you what He has done with the saints who have gone before you — He will change the world. But U got 2 believe!

In this book, Father Stan will give you the keys to this great adventure with Jesus. Perhaps more than any other person I know, Father Stan understands the heart of young people, and he has the gift to communicate the Good News of Jesus Christ.

If you have felt insignificant and view yourself as a no-body, then you're about to meet SOMEBODY that will take the five loaves and two fish of your life and bring them out of hiding into His glorious presence. Prepare to be transformed!

JEFF CAVINS
Host of EWTN's "Life on the Rock"

Introduction

Not My Idea

This book wasn't my idea. Thank you, Jesus! I woke up in the middle of the night with the outline. I wrote it down and put it on the mountain of papers on my desk. I didn't know what it meant.

A few months after this happened, I received an e-mail from Our Sunday Visitor askin me for a manuscript — and here it is! Thanks be to God!

I'd like to thank Mike Dubruiel, everybody at Our Sunday Visitor, and everyone else who encouraged me and helped me to bring this book about.

New Apostolic Outreach

In his message for World Mission Sunday 2001, our Holy Father, Pope John Paul II, said, "A new apostolic outreach is needed . . . taking into account each person's needs in regard to their sensitivity and language."

The linguistic style of this book will include contemporary phrases of urban slang in both content and "spellin." Please know that this is intentional and not the result of poor copyediting!

I'm hopin the language and style will reach out to young and old alike cause I'm tryin to make the book talk — I mean that I'm tryin to write the way I talk.

For those of you who know me, you know what I mean. For those of you who don't know me, I hope you'll get to know what I mean as you read the book! Know what I'm sayin?

How to Use This Book

To get the most out of this book, you will need a Bible and the *Catechism of the Catholic Church*. Many times throughout the book I'm askin you and challengin you to open up the Bible or the "CCC" (my abbreviation for the *Catechism of the Catholic Church*). I hope and pray that you do it!

It's a little extra work, but it will help you to dig more deeply into the Mystery of Christ! Alleluia!

There's a lot of stuff in this book that you can come back to and re-read again and again. I also hope that this book will help you to pray and get close and stay close to Jesus — to know Him, love Him, and serve Him and His Church and all peoples with great love and joy.

There's a lot of spiritual hunger out there today in our youth 4 the truth. I hope and pray this book helps you to feed your soul and many others as well — friends, family, and everybody. Yo, U got 2 believe! Amen!

FATHER STAN FORTUNA, C.F.R.
Feast of St. Anthony of Padua
June 13, 2001

Faith is the assurance of things hoped for, the conviction of things not seen.

Hebrews 11:1

Faith: U Got 2 Believe

A Free Gift!

You've got to believe! What's the point? What's it feel like? What's it gonna do for me? What does it mean? It's hard. . . . I don't understand. . . . Then why? What if . . . I'm afraid. . . .

It's been said that faith is a gift. It is a gift! Faith is a gift from God. The Church teaches that faith is "an entirely free gift that God makes to man" (CCC #162). A gift has to be received. And once it's received, it has to be used — practiced. To practice means to do somethin repeatedly or habitually in order to learn or perfect a skill. So that means every day, every time we feel good or bad, glad or sad, even ferocious or mad, we've got to practice the faith! At least we got to try!

Importance of Faith

Do you know how important faith was in order for Jesus to perform some of His miracles?

Get your Bible out and check out this passage:

➡ Matthew 8:5-13

Jesus heals the centurion's servant.

Jesus was astonished when He saw the faith of a centurion — a Roman official. His servant was paralyzed and in great pain. This centurion guy told Jesus to "only speak the word" because he believed! What did he believe? That his servant would be healed as a result of his faith in Jesus.

Faith Means Trust

When you have faith in a person, you have confidence in that person. Faith involves loyalty. This centurion guy knew all about that. He had a lot of experience, and Jesus was impressed with that. Be sure to read it in the Gospel! Jesus told him, "Go; let it be done for you according to your faith" (Matthew 8:13). His servant was healed at the very hour he spoke with Jesus. He believed! The healing took place without Jesus goin to visit the paralyzed man! U got 2 believe! Things will happen.

The Catholic faith presents us with an awesome opportunity every time we go to Mass and receive Holy Communion.

(And if for whatever reason you can't receive Holy Communion when you go to Mass, maybe because you need to go and make an awesome confession, Jesus is still there and is not bound by that restriction to bless you big time and increase your faith.)

We say the same words as the centurion guy in Matthew 8:5-13. Did you read it yet? Take a break and get to it!

I'm tellin you, if you participate and practice the faith durin Mass you'll never be bored there again. Oh yeah, the music and singin might be borin. Some of the preachin might be borin. The architecture, incense, and lectors may bore you to death — but not your participation in and practice of the faith! You and I will be healed bit by bit, day by day, forever and ever.

Remember, Jesus said whoever eats this bread — referring to the Eucharist — "will live forever" (John 6:51). The power of our faith in Jesus will heal our fear of death and all our fears, and free our hearts and minds for a life of love and service. We're talkin bout the real deal here.

Can You See Faith?

If I could see what faith looks like, then maybe I could believe, right?

Take your Bible out again and check this out:

➡ Mark 2:1-12

Jesus heals a paralyzed man brought to Him by the man's friends.

In Mark 2:1-12, a paralyzed man is brought to Jesus by the man's friends. The crowd was so great that his friends could not carry him in through the door, so it's "up on the roof" they go! Better still, it's through the roof! They made a hole in the roof of the house where Jesus was teachin, and they made lots of noise too! They lowered their paralyzed friend into the room right in front of Jesus. Just imagine the commotion these guys were causin!

St. Mark tells us, "When Jesus saw their faith, he said to the paralytic, 'Son, your sins are forgiven. . . . I say to you, stand up, take your mat and go to your home' " (Mark 2:5, 11). Jesus "saw their faith"!

I thought that faith was bein certain of what we do not see! That's just it! Bein certain of what we do not see but actin on it anyway!

We can't see faith unless it's practiced. It's like the wind. We don't see the wind unless it's blowin and movin something. These guys were so certain that Jesus would heal their friend, they brought him through the roof with their faith and muscle. They didn't see it — they believed it. And guess what? Jesus did it! That's keepin the faith.

Walkin by Faith

We're so bent on seein things — bent right out of shape! The culture of death wants us to walk by sight, not by faith. MTV, videos, the movies, certain songs we listen to, advertisements, and the whole media world — which at times has a good and positive side — do not help us practice the faith.

Remember, the Bible tells us to "walk by faith, not by sight" (2 Corinthians 5:7).

The world and maybe some of your friends (and maybe even some of your family members) would rather have you walk by sight and forget the faith. They might want to bring you up on the roof — not to make an opening to bring you to Jesus, but rather to throw you off! Be careful! Don't worry about your friends, your family, or even yourself! "Fight the good fight, having faith" (1 Timothy 1:18-19).

Do You Lack Faith?

In case you're feelin afraid because of a lack of faith, Jesus has you covered again! "Why are you afraid, you of little faith?" (Matthew 8:26).

Jesus said this to His disciples who woke Him up from a power nap while He was sound asleep in a boat during a violent storm that scared the livin daylights out of them.

Jesus was sleepin peacefully durin the storm. Our faith in Him will empower us to have peace when the troubled waters of life kick in and rock the boat. Know what I'm sayin?

So why are we so afraid durin times of trouble? Maybe you're so afraid that you can't even acknowledge that you really are afraid? Sometimes our biggest problems are due to the fact that we don't know what the problem is.

Don't be afraid. Put your faith in Jesus. He will see you through.

No Faith at All?

Just in case you're feelin like you don't have any faith at all — take it easy! You don't need much faith at all! In fact, a mustard seed is about as big as this dot [.], and Jesus said, "For truly I tell you, if you have faith the size of a mustard seed, you will say to this mountain, 'Move from here to there,' and it will move; and nothing will be impossible for you" (Matthew 17:20).

Now that's power!

Doin the Impossible!

By faith, we share in God's life, and we share in God's power to deal with everything, even the impossible — those things we feel we cannot accomplish, those things that are extremely difficult for us to deal with or tolerate. You know what they are; you know who they are. Or do you know what they are and who they are? Are you ready for a little faith to empower you to start dealin with all of this? Come on . . . U got 2 believe!

Only God is able to deal with all of this, right?

Wrong!

Didn't Jesus say, "For mortals it is impossible, but not for God; for God all things are possible" (Mark 10:27)?

Jesus, because He is true God and true man, empowers us to access the divine power of God by faith! Remember, He said that if we have faith the size of a mustard seed — that's really, really, really small, so He's challengin us by kinda insultin us — then "nothing will be impossible for you." Are you ready for that kind of relationship?

Filial Boldness — Uh . . . What?

By faith, Jesus makes us share in a divine power that belongs only to God. So what kind of relationship are we talkin about? It is a personal relationship between a lovin and all-powerful Father and His children. The relationship between Jesus and His Father, you know: "Our Father who art in heaven. . . ." Now that's what I'm talkin about!

The Church calls this "filial boldness." Check it out:

Catechism of the Catholic Church ➡ #2610

Jesus teaches us to trust God in the same way that He places His total trust in God, and to act believing that God will answer our prayers! Read it — this is important!

Filial boldness — sounds like a big word right? Guess what? *Filial boldness* is a big word because it's a big deal! The deal is this: The personal relationship we can have with our lovin and all-powerful heavenly Father is possible — all because of Jesus.

Check this out! Jesus said: "Very truly, I tell you, the one who believes in me will also do the works that I do and, in fact, will do greater works than these, because I am going to the Father. I will do whatever you ask in my name, so that the Father may be glorified in the Son. If in my name you ask me for anything, I will do it" (John 14:12-14).

It's really amazin! Because of our faith in Jesus, we actually can do the works that Jesus did. And not only do the works Jesus did, but even greater. Awesome!

But . . .

But do ya know what the problem is? Most of us don't really practice the faith every day, so we don't grow in the faith, and the result is we stay at the same old level of faith. Imagine if we took our faith life seriously every day, the same way we take care of our bodies? Most of us don't even do that well, but we do eat, drink, and sleep every day.

What if we really had a strong awareness experience and a feelin of bein a child of God, that God is *my* Father, the Creator of the universe — every day, not just on Sundays or even once in a while? Maybe even just one time — to have a really strong experience that God is *my* Father!

Were talkin bout the real deal here. Now wait a minute. You might be sayin, "Hey, Fadda [that's Bronxeese for Father], don't take this 'filial boldness' thing too seriously. Take it easy!"

Well, check this out! Go back a few paragraphs and re-read John 14:12-14 again. Now that's pretty awesome!

Faith and Works?

Wait a minute. Did I hear somebody say "faith and works"?

There have been such problems contributing to the sad division of the Body of Christ in the sad history of the Christian faith with this "faith and works" thing. O Lord, have mercy! There's enough stuff to do a whole book just on that alone, and it's been done before. It's all about faith, right?

St. Paul talks about the righteousness that is revealed from God, a righteousness that is revealed by faith from first to last, just as it is written: "The one who is righteous will live by faith" (Romans 1:17).

In Romans 3:28, he says, "For we hold that a person is justified by faith apart from works prescribed by the law." In verse 31, he makes himself clear by askin, "Do we then overthrow the law by this faith? By no means! On the contrary, we uphold the law."

Yet when it came to the money collection, St. Paul was speakin like an ambassador for the greatest nation in the universe with one word summin up the message: donation.

Listen to what St. Paul says to the community at Corinth: "Now as you excel in everything — in faith, in speech, in knowledge, in utmost eagerness, and in our love for you — so we want you to excel also in this generous undertaking. I do not say this as a command, but I am testing the genuineness of your love against the earnestness of others" (2 Corinthians 8:7-8).

I don't know about you, but to me it sounds like works with faith, and with the collection basket! My, oh my, how some things never change! Yet at the same time, there's a real connection between the collection basket and the faith. It ain't all about money; it's all about the faith in our hearts and how we live that faith out every day followin Jesus. That's the deal — Jesus is the Deal . . . the Real Deal.

Faith Expresses Itself in Love

In Galatians 5:6, St. Paul says, "The only thing that counts is faith working through love." And in the same Letter to the

Galatians, he still emphasizes the absolute importance of faith alone in tons of other places. Yet that faith expressin itself through love kinda sounds like works, doesn't it?

Well, what about Ephesians 2:8-9, where he says, "By grace you have been saved through faith, and this is not your own doing; it is the gift of God — not the result of works, so that no one may boast." Here we go again, sounds like a problem with works and faith, right? Let's keep goin!

St. Paul was prayin and thankin God for the people in Colossae because he had heard of their faith in Christ Jesus and the love they had for all the saints (see Colossians 1:5). To the community in Thessalonica, he prayed again for the people because of their faith, hope, and love. It's all connected — yes, faith, and yes, works (see 1 Thessalonians 1:3).

Works produced by faith! Got to have it! The "it" is a "them" — faith and works. Works can't save us and neither can faith without works, and the greatest work is love.

In 2 Thessalonians 1:3 St. Paul thanked God for the community there because of their faith and love. He said, "We must always give thanks to God for you, brothers and sisters, as is right, because your faith is growing abundantly, and the love of everyone of you for one another is increasing." In 2 Thessalonians 1:12, he was very pleased with their acts that were prompted by faith. Are you gettin it yet?

When he wrote to Timothy regarding the command of faith he said, "The aim of such instruction is love that comes from a pure heart, a good conscience, and sincere faith" (1 Timothy 1:5).

Faith in Action

If you want to see a long list of faith in action, be sure to take a break here and open up your Bible to Chapter 11 of the Letter to the Hebrews. What an awesome cloud of witnesses! You'll read about Abel and his pleasing sacrifice to God. In Hebrews 11:4, we are told that "he died, but through his faith he still speaks." Now that's awesome!

And what about Enoch? The Bible says, "By faith Enoch was taken so that he did not experience death" (Hebrews 11:5). (Now this is a really cool verse to use when someone wants to argue against the Assumption of the Blessed Mother. Yeah!) Now that's really awesome! You'll read about Noah, Abraham, Isaac, Jacob, Joseph, Moses, and even "Rahab the prostitute" (Hebrews 11:31), as well as Gideon, Barak, Samson, Jephthah, David, Samuel and the prophets.

Through faith, all these people conquered kingdoms, administered justice, and gained what was promised. They shut the mouths of lions, quenched the fury of the flames, and escaped the edge of the sword. Their weakness was turned to strength. And they became powerful in battle and routed foreign armies. Women received back their dead — raised to life!

Others were tortured and refused to be released, so that they might gain a better resurrection. Some faced jeers and flogging, while still others were chained and put in prison. They were stoned. They were sawed in two. They were put to death by the sword. They went about in sheepskins and goatskins, destitute, persecuted, and mistreated.

What could make any of this possible? Faith! Are you ready for some of that? U got 2 believe!

Actions Speak Louder Than Words!

The real bottom-line witness of the faith comes from St. James, who kinda sums up the whole deal between faith and works. "What good is it, my brothers and sisters, if you say you have faith but do not have works? Can faith save you?" (James 2:14). Then St. James goes into the whole deal about a brother or sister who needs food or clothing and nothin is done to help them in their need but they are told, "Go in peace; keep warm and eat your fill" (James 2:16). In James 2:17, he says, "So faith by itself, if it has no works, is dead."

So it is possible that we can have faith — but please, Lord, make sure it's not a dead faith! Make it alive with the love, power, and good deeds that flow from the gifts and power of the Holy Spirit!

St. James continues, "But someone will say, 'You have faith and I have works.' Show me your faith apart from your works, and I by my works will show you my faith" (James 2:18).

And check it out, as St. James reaches a grand finale (James 2:20-26):

> Do you want to be shown, you senseless person, that faith apart from works is barren? Was not our ancestor Abraham justified by works when he offered his son Isaac on the altar? You see that faith was active along with his works, and faith was brought to completion by the works. Thus the scripture was fulfilled that says, "Abraham believed God, and it was reckoned to him as righteousness," and he was called the friend of God. You see that a person is justified by works and not by faith alone. Likewise, was not Rahab the prostitute also justified by works when she welcomed the messengers and sent them out by another road? For just as the body without the spirit is dead, so faith without works is also dead.

So, you might be askin, what's the point?

Faith — An Awesome Gift!

We have such an awesome gift, this faith. We need to pray, pray, pray . . . start a prayer life, renew our prayer life, and grow in our prayer life to increase our faith life and the power that's available to us, right there inside of our hearts. You want some of that? Open your heart — trust, surrender, believe, and receive.

St. Paul wanted some of that and got it! As we say in our neighborhood, he had some "mad" filial boldness! That means he had a lot of filial boldness! He said, "I can do all things through him who strengthens me" (Philippians 4:13). He said it because he believed it — and because he believed it, he had the experience.

The Power of Faith

Did you know that Evander Holyfield had "Philippians 4:13" written on his boxin trunks when he defeated Mike Tyson for the World Heavyweight Championship title? Don't be fooled: It wasn't the writin on his trunks that gave him the courage, strength, and discipline to achieve his goal; it was the faith in his heart, which the written words symbolized.

At the time, most people thought a victory for Holyfield against Tyson was close to impossible. Remember, Jesus told us that if we have the smallest amount of faith, nothin will be impossible for us. Holyfield believed and won!

Speakin about the impossible, how about Peter walkin on the water?

Check this out:

➡ Matthew 14:22-33

Jesus and Peter take a stroll on the lake.

Now this is somethin (walkin on water) that we wouldn't want to try on our own to practice the faith. But Jesus called Peter to take that huge step of faith, and there he was — walkin on the water!

But when Peter started thinkin about how strong the wind was and stopped believin, he did two things. First, he started to sink, and then he got Jesus really bugged! Then Jesus did two things. First, as Peter was sinkin and screamin "Lord, save me!" Jesus "immediately reached out his hand and caught him." The second thing was that Jesus reprimanded Peter and said, "You of little faith, why did you doubt?" (Matthew 14:30-31).

Why Do We Doubt?

Jesus' question is a good one for us to pray with: Why do we doubt? It's certainly easier to doubt than it is to believe. Yet, why do we doubt? Let's take that one to prayer.

Remember, in the Gospel, Jesus didn't just get bugged with Peter and reprimand him because he doubted; no, Jesus also prayed for Peter. He prayed that Peter's faith would not fail, probably because He saw how far Peter was willin to go in trustin Him — like steppin out in faith by gettin out of a perfectly good boat and onto the water and walkin!

Check this out: "Simon, Simon, listen! Satan has demanded to sift all of you like wheat, but I have prayed for you that your own faith may not fail; and you, when once you have turned back, strengthen your brothers" (Luke 22:31-32).

Jesus tells us that faith can weaken. That means faith must be strengthened. Jesus prays for Peter's faith to be strong so he can go and strengthen the faith of his brothers.

Take Steps to Strengthen Your Faith!

See what's goin on here? What's that mean for you? What are you doin to strengthen your faith?

1. **Are you reading your Bible every day?** Wait a minute, do you even have your own Bible? How about at least goin over the readings for Sunday Mass? Are you goin to Mass?
2. **Do you pray to Mary our Blessed Mother and ask her to help your faith increase?**
3. **Do you spend time or make a little visit once in a while to Jesus in the Blessed Sacrament — the Sacrament of faith?** If Jesus prayed for Peter's faith not to fail, we can count on Jesus prayin for our faith to be strong. Then others can count on us to be there for them, standin strong on the Rock and keepin the faith. Amen?

Reachin Out 2 Believe

One of my favorite stories in the Gospel is the woman who touched the edge of Jesus' cloak. She's awesome!

Check her out in:

➡ Mark 5:24-34

A woman reaches out in faith to touch Jesus.

This woman believed — in other words, she had faith and practiced it! She just knew that if she just touched the cloak of Jesus, she would be healed. So what did she do?

The woman snuck up behind Jesus, who was standin in a huge crowd, and touched the edge of His cloak, all the time believin that Jesus could and would heal her. And BOOM! As soon as she touched His cloak, her blood flow dried up and she felt in her body that she was healed of her affliction. St. Mark tells us, "Immediately aware that power had gone forth from him, Jesus turned around in the crowd and said, 'Who touched my clothes?' " (Mark 5:30).

The woman was afraid.

No kiddin! Could you imagine havin Jesus lookin for you because divine power was released by you because you believed and touched His cloak? She finally fessed up and came to Jesus, fell down before Him, and "told him the whole truth" (Mark 5:33).

That's a great piece of advice — to come to Jesus and tell Him the whole truth!

She must have said somethin like this: "Jesus, I'm so sorry! I just knew, I believed with all my heart and mind, that if I just touched your cloak, I could be healed."

And what do you think Jesus said to her? "You should have asked me first! Don't disrespect my divine power! I had a whole list of people who I was plannin to heal first! You jumped the line! Gimme that healin back!"

No! No! No! In fact, Jesus said to her, "Daughter, your faith has made you well; go in peace, and be healed of your disease" (Mark 5:34).

"Daughter, your faith has made you well." *Your* faith! How awesome! Are you aware that your faith in Jesus can save? That's what your faith is all about. Are you gettin it yet? I'm still workin on it. Don't worry: It's a lifetime journey. You want some of that peace and healin? Believe — give your heart to Jesus and let your faith save you too!

When Jesus Returns, Will He Find Faith?

This faith thing is so crucial. St. Paul said, "Now faith, hope, and love abide, these three; and the greatest of these is love" (1 Corinthians 13:13).

We've got to love one another as Jesus loved us, especially if we "got plans" to go to heaven. You can be sure that without faith in Jesus, there ain't no way we will be able to love one another as He loved us. In fact, in Luke 18:8, Jesus asks a kind of ultimate question: "And yet, when the Son of Man comes, will he find faith on earth?" That's big! Will He find faith in me? Will He find faith in you? I hope so! I believe so! Amen!

In Matthew 24:12, Jesus said, "Because of the increase of lawlessness, the love of many will grow cold." Remember, love is the greatest! So if an increase of evil-doin will make love grow cold, then an increase of faith will set love into a ragin fire energizin us to persevere to the end, to keep on goin. To have faith in Jesus right up till He comes again in glory or if we die before He comes — that's what I'm talkin about!

Either way, it won't matter. Nothin will matter because our faith will be strong, and Jesus will bless us with that peace that is beyond understandin. That's why the Bible tells us, "Do not worry about anything, but in everything by prayer and supplication with thanksgiving let your requests be made known to God. And the peace of God, which surpasses all understanding, will guard your hearts and minds in Christ Jesus" (Philippians 4:6-7).

Faith Can Be Lost

The Tradition of our Church teaches us somethin that's really important. We can lose this priceless gift of faith.

Check this out: To live, grow, and persevere in the faith until the end:

1. We must nourish it with the Word of God.
2. We must ask the Lord to increase our faith: "I believe; help my unbelief!" (Mark 9:24); "Increase our faith!" (Luke 17:5).
3. We must be "working through charity," abounding in hope, and rooted in the faith of the Church.

What are some of the things that can help to weaken the faith? Watch out for "voluntary doubt." That's when we disregard, when we do not pay attention to or neglect what God has revealed, or what the Church puts forth for us to believe. And watch out for "involuntary doubt." That's when we hesitate, hold back in doubt or indecision, regardin things connected with the faith. This kind-a-thing can cause spiritual blindness.

Check it out:

Catechism of the Catholic Church ➡ #2088-2089

There are various forms of spiritual blindness.

Don't be fooled to think just because "I believe," that life will be easy. God will give us all that we need to march on and to fight the good fight and be victorious! But remember, a fight is a fight and will require us to do battle and put forth a determined effort, to carry on, to struggle, endure, persevere — to stay close to Jesus.

Check out what the Church teaches:

Catechism of the Catholic Church ➡ #164

There are a lot of things in life that can test our faith and tempt us to doubt!

The Church Is the Mother of Faith

"Faith comes from what is heard, and what is heard comes through the word of Christ" (Romans 10:17). The Word of Christ comes from the Bible, and the Bible comes from the Church. So the Church is the mother of faith and the teacher of the faith and the guardian of the faith.

Read this:

Catechism of the Catholic Church ➡ #169

The Church is our mother and our teacher.

St. Paul the Apostle talks about receivin the grace to be chosen an apostle from Jesus "to bring about the obedience of faith . . . for the sake of his name" (Romans 1:5), in the beginning of his great Letter to the Romans.

In the conclusion, St. Paul puts it like this in Romans 16:25-27:

> Now to God who is able to strengthen you according to my gospel and the proclamation of Jesus Christ, according to the revelation of the mystery that was kept secret for long ages but is now disclosed, and through the prophetic writings is made known to all the Gentiles, according to the command of the eternal God, to bring about

the obedience of faith — to the only wise God, through
Jesus Christ, to whom be the glory forever! Amen."

We Need Help!

To obey is rooted in the Latin word *ob-audire*, which means
to hear or to loosen. To obey in faith means to "submit freely
to the word that has been heard, because its truth is guaran-
teed by God who is Truth itself" (CCC #144).

Remember, earlier on we talked about faith as bein a free
gift God gives to us and that we have to practice it. We need
help! Can you say amen to that? Don't you find it to be so true
that we need help? Admittin to that is a lot easier to do than
to actually ask for help — help from others and especially
from the Lord! Even though there is a dimension of faith that
is a human act, we need the grace of God to pull the whole
thing off.

Check this out:

Catechism of the Catholic Church ➡ #153

*We need a lot of help before faith can be practiced,
not just from others but from God too!*

We Need the Holy Spirit!

Yet, at the same time, while practicin the faith is only possible by the workin of the Holy Spirit in our heart, mind, and
soul, the Church teaches that the act of faith is truly a human
act. (Check out CCC #153. C'mon, have U read it yet?). We've
seen so many examples of this in the Gospel and hope to see
plenty more in the lives of each one of you! Join the great
cloud of witnesses who have marched on, keepin the faith. If
you want to join the saints when they go "marchin in," you've
got to keep on "marchin on" in the faith.

Witnesses of Faith

Abraham is our father of faith. St. Paul said, "he is the father of all of us" (Romans 4:16). Our Blessed Mother Mary is "its most perfect embodiment" (CCC #144). Remember, Jesus said, "The one who endures to the end will be saved" (Matthew 24:13) and "The one who believes and is baptized will be saved; but the one who does not believe will be condemned" (Mark 16:16).

Maybe you haven't had any good witnesses of faith in your life; be a good witness to the faith and stand firm keepin the faith. Maybe you had some great witnesses to the faith. If so, can you identify them?

I immediately think of my grandparents: Greek Orthodox and Italian Roman Catholics. What a combo! I'm truly grateful to the Lord for them and for my parents who handed down their good example to me.

Your parents were suppose ta be that witness to you and teach you the faith — first, by their example. If you didn't get that, don't worry; be that for others, especially if you get married and are blessed with children.

Read this:

Catechism of the Catholic Church   ➡ **#2226**

The Church teaches the importance of parents giving the faith to their children! U might read this to your parents!

Passing on the Faith

Maybe you need to transmit the faith to your parents, brothers, sisters, relatives, and friends! Maybe they've been tryin to do that to you — whatever! No one can do it alone!

Long ago God spoke to our ancestors in many and various ways by the prophets, but in these last days he has spoken to us by a Son.

Hebrews 1:1-2

CHAPTER 2

Revelation: Yo, It Ain't Me!

What Is Revelation?

Revelation is all about God coming to us, reachin out to us, communicatin with us, makin Himself known — His name, His love, His will, His mystery. . . .

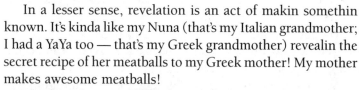

Brother Webster (my name for the dictionary) defines revelation *as an act of revealin or communicatin divine truth, somethin that is revealed by God to humans.*

In a lesser sense, revelation is an act of makin somethin known. It's kinda like my Nuna (that's my Italian grandmother; I had a YaYa too — that's my Greek grandmother) revealin the secret recipe of her meatballs to my Greek mother! My mother makes awesome meatballs!

The focus here is another big word, *divine revelation*, which means how God makes Himself known to us.

Check it out:

In His goodness and wisdom, God chose to reveal Himself and to make known to us the hidden purpose of His will (cf. Eph. 1:9) by which through Christ, the Word made flesh, man has access to the Father in the Holy Spirit and comes to share in the divine nature (cf. Eph. 2:18, 2 Pet. 1:4). Through this revelation, therefore, the invisible God (cf. Col. 1:15; 1 Tim. 1:17) out of the abundance of His love speaks to men as friends (cf. Ex. 33:11; Jn. 15:14-15) and lives among them (cf. Bar. 3:38), so that He may invite and take them into fellowship with Himself.

— Dogmatic Constitution on Divine Revelation #2

'Yo! It Ain't Me'

The bottom line of divine revelation is "Yo! It ain't me." We see this in the revelation to a young man named Samuel in the Old Testament in the First Book of Samuel, Chapter 3.

Get your Bible out and check out this passage:

➡ 1 Samuel 3

God reveals Himself to Samuel.

Samuel was sound asleep when he heard someone callin his name. So what did he do?

He got up and went to Eli, the old priest who was also sleepin nearby. Eli told him to go back to sleep. Kinda like "Kid, you're just dreamin, go back to sleep!"

Samuel thought it was Eli calling him, and Eli told him, " Yo! It ain't me."

So Samuel goes back to sleep and again hears someone callin him. He gets up and goes to Eli a second time, and Eli tells him again, " Look dude, it ain't me callin you. Go back to sleep!"

The Bible tells us, "Samuel did not yet know the Lord, and the word of the Lord had not yet been revealed to him" (1 Samuel 3:7). We recognize the voices of those we know, but we don't recognize the voices of people we do not know. Samuel didn't know the Lord, so of course he didn't know it was Him that was doin the callin.

The same thing happens a third time! The Lord called Samuel, who went to Eli, and Eli told him, "Go, lie down; and if he calls you, you shall say, 'Speak, LORD, for your servant is listening' " (1 Samuel 3:9).

So Samuel went back to sleep for the fourth time! And finally the Lord came and revealed His presence, callin out as before, "Samuel! Samuel!" And Samuel said, "Speak, for your servant is listening" (1 Samuel 3:10).

Finally, he got the point. It wasn't him. It wasn't Eli. It was the Lord — God!

God Revealin Himself

The reality and mystery of God revealin Himself, makin Himself known to us, is *divine revelation*. This is what was happenin to Samuel. Once he figured out that it wasn't Eli, and Eli guided him to understand that it might be God, he was ready to open himself up to the reality of God's revelation — divine revelation.

It is the same with us! We might not know God, so if He calls us we probably aren't goin to recognize His voice. Divine revelation is not just a head-trip of theological doctrine and dogma. Doctrine and dogma can help us to know about God and even prepare the way for us to recognize Him when He is present. But we need to be expectant and open, allowin God to interrupt our plans and to erupt in our lives. Like Samuel!

He was enjoyin a good night's sleep. The last thing he wanted was someone to be wakin him up!

What about you?

What if God was to wake you up in the middle of the night? Would you say, "Speak, Lord, for your servant is listenin?" Or would you say, "Yo, shut up, I'm tryin to sleep. Come back later!"

I'm sure, if you knew it was the Lord, you'd never say, "Yo, shut up!" You don't really wanna talk that way to anybody, right?

But of course this is exactly the point. If you really understand how God works, you can never know who it might be that is callin your name. But you can bet on God being present

24/7, so we've got to do our best always to do our best, and to be open to God — know what I'm sayin?

Knock, Knock! Who's There?

What if God were to interrupt your very life, let alone your sleep? What if God were to erupt in your life? A visit from God might stop whatever it is we may be doin at the time and "break in," even like a thief in the night.

God might break into our sleepin to wake us up, to break into our sinnin to get us to stop, to set us free, or even break into the most important things or people in our lives accordin to His mysterious purpose. Or He may even erupt in our lives and burst us free from all that stuff that we call weakness, our limits, or whatever or whoever holds us back. Are you ready for some of that? Are you ready for revelation?

Do Ya Wanna Feel the Power of the Holy Spirit?

When we open our hearts to God, God will send us the Holy Spirit. When this happens, we become personally involved with what I call the "bustin-out" power of the Holy Spirit.

This is a line from my CD Take My Heart, *and the song titled the same. Check it out:*

You gotta learn how to pray if ya wanna feel the Power,
Go to Church, settle down, make ya self a Holy Hour.
Let Him take your heart.

Revelation is not just about information; it's about a personal relationship with God. And when we have that relationship, God gives us His Spirit — the Holy Spirit! So our lives breathe with new life, God's life! This unleashes the "bustin-out" power of God within us!

It's too bad that most Catholics (some young and some old) don't know how to access that power. Ya figya they would! That's what the Sacrament of Confirmation is all about — and is able to do for us. Not unleashin this power is like being sick, havin a prescription that can make you well but never goin to the drugstore to fill it! Know what I'm sayin?

The day of Pentecost revealed the mystery and power of the Holy Spirit and the change that it can make in a person's life. Take a break here, get your Bible, and read the Chapter 2 of Acts.

Open your Bible and check this out:

➡ Acts 2

This is what happens when the Holy Spirit comes into our lives.

Have you read it yet? Does it sound like what happened to you on the day of your confirmation? Are you out preachin what God has done for you, or are you afraid? Are you livin in the way the early Christians did — sharin what they had with one another — or are you holdin back, worried you won't have enough? Are you still "waitin" to feel that power?

In 1998, on Pentecost Sunday, my personal hero, our Holy Father, Pope John Paul II, said this about the Holy Spirit. Check it out!

The Holy Spirit extends the mission of Christ the Lord in time and space. The Spirit thus makes the Church a stream of new life that flows through the history of mankind. . . . There is so much need today for mature Christian personalities, conscious of their baptismal identity, of their vocation and mission in the Church and world.

We might be so lazy and sluggish in our relationship with God that He might have to come lookin like a tongue of fire about to set down on our heads — that would get us movin!

Now that's revelation!

Do You Know Him Yet?

Our problem might be like that of young Samuel. Do you remember what his problem was? Did you read it?

Samuel was not familiar with the Lord. Are you?

God ain't a bully or a thug, yet He certainly doesn't want you sleepwalkin through life as a member of the livin dead! He wants you to be with Him, fully alive, now and forever. When God interrupts and erupts in your life, it's awesome. He helps us to grow up, to mature, to go deeper in our relationship with Him, with ourselves, and then with others so we can reveal His love and goodness to others after we first get it ourselves. Get it?

The Holy Spirit can reveal to us and help us to experience "the breadth and length and height and depth, and to know the love of Christ that surpasses knowledge" (Ephesians 3:18-19).

My Conversion

I wasn't born a priest. It took a long time before I finally gave the Lord permission to break into my life, to interrupt and erupt, settin me free to say yes to Him. There's nothin like it!

It's been many years since my conversion began, and God still interrupts me and my plans with His plans — every day!

What at first seems to be an interruption is actually an intervention — God comin between whoever or whatever I may be experiencin or goin through. There are my plans and then there are His plans — and there's usually a big difference between the two!

The old sayin holds true: "Man proposes and God disposes."

How did it all get started? It was the power of God revealin Himself in His Word through a Catholic Bible-study group that was the key to my initial conversion, and it's His Word that still keeps me goin! The Word of God in the Bible not only revealed God to me but also revealed me to me.

Check it out what the Letter to the Hebrews tells us:

Indeed, the word of God is living and active, sharper than any two-edged sword, piercing until it divides soul from spirit, joints from marrow; it is able to judge the thoughts and intentions of the heart.

— *Hebrews 4:12*

That's my heart! Once my heart is opened by His grace, I'm ready for His Heart, His Love for me, and His Will for me. There's nothin like it — and nothin else matters. Trust me! It's awesome! He's awesome! Trust Him and you'll see for yourself.

What About You?

God speaks powerfully in His Word in the Scriptures. The Bible and His Word can be revealed everywhere and in everyone if He so chooses! We heard about young Samuel's experience, and I told you a little about mine. Now what about you?

Have you ever had the experience of God revealin Himself to you? That's a critical experience for you to have in order to cash in on the fullness of your Catholic faith! You have to submit yourself to the lovin and powerful authority of our heavenly Father, His Son, the Holy Spirit, and His Church. Listen to what the Church teaches.

Check this out. This is awesome:

In the sacred books, the Father who is in heaven meets His children with great love and speaks with them; and the force and power in the word of God is so great that it remains the support and energy of the Church, the strength of faith for her sons, the food of the soul, the pure and perennial source of spiritual life.

— *Dogmatic Constitution on Divine Revelation* #21

You can see that the Holy Scriptures are the place for us to meet God, and indeed that was the case for me! So what about you? Don't you want to meet Him too and experience His power?

Even if and when we have a sense of what's happenin with revealed truth because of our natural reason — our ability to think — it ain't us! It's all about God!

Accordin to St. Thomas Aquinas, when we have a sense of what's happenin, it's "because of the authority of God Himself who reveals."

Check it out:

Catechism of the Catholic Church ➡ #156

It's the authority of God that leads us to belief.

So we can see right off the bat that divine revelation is goin to be a problem for some people because it involves authority. Most of us — in fact, all of us, to a greater or lesser degree — have some kind of problem with authority.

Problems With Authority

Stop and think about it. Who likes authority? Who likes people to be in command over us? Who likes it when their parents or grandparents tell us "Don't wear this!" or "Don't do that!" or "Do this!" or "Be home on time!" or "Don't go here (or there)!" or "I don't want you hangin out with so and so!"?

Who likes the cop who gives us a ticket for speedin? Who likes the teacher who tells us to stop talkin in class and assigns all those pages to read over the weekend?

Who likes the Church when she tells us what to do and what not to do?

Even the authority of God over our lives and our choices — who likes it?

We see this especially in the area of morality. We have a whole chapter on morality comin up next. We kinda have a natural resistance to any power or influence or command imposed upon us — and understandably so!

I think our dislike of authority is really a fear of authority, a fear of not bein in control.

St. Paul helps us resolve the dilemma: "Do you wish to have no fear of the authority? Then do what is good, and you will receive its approval" (Romans 13:3). He also said that "whoever resists authority resists what God has appointed, and those who resist will incur judgment." (Romans 13:2).

When Authority Is Welcomed

There is a dimension of authority that's attractive. Think about the times when there has been a problem of some type. Have you ever been involved in a minor car accident and it wasn't your fault? Aren't you glad to see the cops pull up in the patrol car?

What about when the teacher calls you to the desk and authorizes you to leave the classroom to run an errand? Oh yeah, bet you like that! Then authority feels a little different because it's in your favor.

But don't be fooled. Lawful authority is in your favor even when you get caught doin somethin that's wrong, even though it doesn't feel that way! Remember, authority has a positive dimension to it, especially when we see it in the life of Jesus.

The people who had the awesome privilege to see and hear Jesus preach felt His authority and were amazed by it. St. Matthew tells us, "The crowds were astounded at his teaching, for he taught them as one having authority, and not as their scribes" (Matthew 7:28-29).

The people saw this revelation of Jesus as somethin new, causin them to wonder, "What is this? A new teaching — with authority!" (Mark 1:27).

While some people were amazed by Jesus' teachin, others were angered. This was most true when Jesus talked about His power to forgive sins. The teachers of the law couldn't take it! This dimension — forgivin sins — revealed the divine nature of Jesus' authority and His Person. Jesus is a divine Person. This really drove the "authorities" crazy!

Real-Deal Authority — The Son of God!

When Jesus healed the paralytic, He said to him, "Take heart, son; your sins are forgiven" (Matthew 9:2).

Get your Bible out and check out this passage:

➡ Matthew 9:3-8

Jesus has the authority to forgive and heal.

Later in the Gospel of Matthew, the authority of Jesus is once again questioned. The chief priests and elders were really bugged with Jesus. Notice how the Lord puts them right in their place.

Open your Bible and check this out. It is so cool:

➡ Matthew 21:23-27

Ain't no trippin up Jesus.

We've got to learn from Jesus. There's a way to deal with authority and a way not to. Jesus respected them but would not allow their deceit to deter Him and hold Him back.

Just think about if the chief priests and elders answered Jesus' question about the origin of John's baptism. I'm sure

Jesus would have revealed a whole lot more to them, and their anger would have turned into a rage. It happens!

Tired of Payin Taxes?

Once again, in Luke's Gospel, the deceitful authorities sent spies to try to catch Jesus in preaching errors so that they could have Him arrested. Jesus was so cool in dealin with these sneaks. He stayed calm, cool, and collected. May He help us to do the same!

Open your Bible and check out:

➡ Luke 20:20-26

What will Jesus say about payin taxes?

These lawful and awful authorities really frustrated Jesus.

Temple of God or the Local Mall?

In John 2:13-22, when it was almost Passover, Jesus went up to Jerusalem. He entered the Temple and found venders sellin cattle, sheep, and doves. People were also exchangin money — and Jesus threw a holy fit!

St. John tells us, "Making a whip of cords, he drove all of them out of the temple, both the sheep and the cattle. He also poured out the coins of the money changers and overturned their tables. He told those who were selling the doves, 'Take these things out of here! Stop making my Father's house a marketplace!" (John 2:15-16).

Jesus was revealin His divine authority here. The Bible has plenty to reveal about God's wrath, and we get a taste of it here in Jesus turnin over the tables and physically expressin His righteous anger and frustration. Could you imagine what Jesus looked like when He did this? Boy, I sure don't want Jesus mad at me! Talk about revelation as a type of eruption!

Once the dust settled, the local authorities demanded an explanation from Jesus. They asked Him, "What sign can you show us for doing this?" (John 2:18).

When Jesus answered them, He revealed somethin awesome about His divine Person and His mission. He said, "Destroy this temple, and in three days I will raise it up" (John 2:19).

They immediately start arguin about how long it took to build the Temple, but St. John clears up the confusion and manifests the revelation of the mystery of Jesus and His resurrection by sayin, "But he was speaking of the temple of his body" (John 2:21). After He was raised from the dead, the Scriptures tell us that the disciples remembered what He had said and they believed! Do U? U got 2!

Many Believed in His Name

After the dramatic episode of Jesus cleanin out the Temple, St. John tells us that "many believed in his name because they saw the signs that he was doing" (John 2:23). Then he reveals somethin very interestin about Jesus and the people who saw His miracles. He says, "But Jesus on his part would not entrust himself to them, because he knew all people and needed no one to testify about anyone; for he himself knew what was in everyone" (John 2:24-25).

To come to know Jesus is the surest way to come to know ourselves. This is one of the most awesome and beautiful dimensions of divine revelation. It's kinda like Carvel ice cream on Wednesdays — where I live they have a two-for-one special, buy one and get one free. When we come to know and experience the mystery of God as He reveals Himself in Jesus, we also will come to know ourselves. What an awesome journey!

Jesus Fully Reveals Himself to the Church

As Catholics, we have the fullness of revelation because God has fully revealed Himself in Jesus, and Jesus fully reveals Himself to us in His Church. Yet in order for us to be able to receive this revelation of the mystery and meanin of our humanity, it is critical that we grow into the fullness of Jesus Himself.

We need to acknowledge that "he [God] has put all things under his [Jesus'] feet and has made him the head over all things for the church, which is his body, the fullness of him who fills all in all" (Ephesians 1:22-23). Jesus is the only way you and I can come to understand ourselves more completely.

The followin quotation from Pope John Paul II is so awesome that you will want to read and re-read it again and again. Every time I read it, it moves me deeply and inspires me to do what it says — to draw near to Jesus:

The man who wishes to understand himself thoroughly — and not just in accordance with immediate, partial, often superficial, and even illusory standards and measures of his being — he must with his unrest, uncertainty, and even his weakness and sinfulness, with his life and death, draw near to Christ. He must, so to speak, enter into him with all his own self, he must "appropriate" *[this is a cool word — it means to take exclusive possession of, to make your very own, to set aside for a particular use or purpose]* and assimilate *[here's another cool word — it means to absorb into the system, to take into the mind and really understand]* the whole of the reality of the Incarnation and Redemption in order to find himself. If this profound process takes place within him, he then bears fruit not only of adoration of God but also of deep wonder at himself. How precious must man be in the eyes of the Creator, if he "gained so great a Redeemer" and if God "gave his only Son in order that man should not perish but have eternal life" (cf. Jn 3:16).

— *The Redeemer of Man #10*

This is not simply about knowledge but about a dynamic and personal relationship with a person, the Person of Jesus Christ.

A Relationship With Jesus

Can you say that you have a personal relationship with Jesus? Maybe you can "say" that, but do you actually have a personal relationship with Jesus?

Even if it's not the most perfect relationship, let it be real and sincere. If you think you don't have a relationship with Jesus, let's pray right now as you're readin this book and ask Him to come into your heart. Even if you've asked Him a thousand times, let's ask Him "one mo time."

Prayer for a Personal Relationship With Jesus

Lord Jesus, come into my heart,
Reveal the Mystery of Yourself to me,
The Mystery of the Heart of the Father,
The Love of the Holy Spirit.
In Your mercy
Forgive me my sins.
Reveal me to me
So I can give myself to You,
As You give Yourself to me,
For my well-being and salvation,
So I can make a more complete
And perfect gift of myself
In loving service to all my brothers and sisters.
Lord Jesus, I trust in You.
Amen.

This is what I was talkin bout earlier, how the Word of God reveals the thoughts and intentions of the heart — my heart that is!

(Check out Hebrews 4:12: "Indeed, the word of God is living and active, sharper than any two-edged sword, piercing until it divides soul from spirit, joints from marrow; it is able to judge the thoughts and intentions of the heart." I put it here just in case you're gettin a little lazy!)

Jesus Shows Us Who We Really Are

This is a beautiful way to see how Scripture and Tradition work together to bring us the fullness of divine revelation. That's what's so cool about bein Catholic! The Church teaches us that Jesus, true God and true man, doesn't just reveal God to us, but that He also reveals us to ourselves — He reveals me to me. He can reveal you to you too! He reveals the thoughts and reflections of not only His Heart, but my heart and your heart, our hearts, and all hearts!

Check out this awesome teachin from the Second Vatican Council:

Only in the mystery of the incarnate Word does the mystery of man take on light. For Adam, the first man, was a figure of Him who was to come (cf. Rom. 5:14), namely, Christ the Lord. Christ, the final Adam, by the revelation of the mystery of the Father and His love, fully reveals man to man himself and makes his supreme calling clear. . . . He who is the "image of the invisible God" (Col. 1:15) is Himself the perfect man. To the sons of Adam He restores the divine likeness which had been disfigured from the first sin onward. Since human nature as He assumed it was not annulled, by that very fact it has been raised up to a divine dignity in our respect too. For by His incarnation the Son of God has united Himself in some fashion with every man. He worked with human hands, He thought with a human mind, acted by human choice, and loved with a human heart. Born of the Virgin

Mary, He has truly been made one of us, like us in all things except sin.

— Pastoral Constitution on the Church in the Modern World #22

Pope John Paul II, buildin on this awesome teachin in his first encyclical letter, *The Redeemer of Man*, puts it this way: "In Christ and through Christ God has revealed himself fully to mankind and has definitively drawn close to it; at the same time, in Christ and through Christ man has acquired full awareness of his dignity, of the heights to which he is raised, of the surpassing worth of his own humanity, and of the meaning of his existence" (#11).

Don't Let the Devil Rule!

I don't mean to beat a dead horse, so I won't. But this authority thing is huge. It's not just somethin that can get you bugged and frustrated.

Open up your Bible and check this out:

➡ Luke 4:1-13

Jesus is tempted by the devil.

Don't forget that authority was used by the devil to tempt Jesus. And if the devil used it to tempt Jesus, don't you be fooled to think for one minute that the devil can't and won't use authority to tempt you. In an instant, he can fool you with his slick and subtle lies, givin you good reasons to do really stupid, harmful, and sinful things. So be careful — really, really careful.

Pray for protection. Pray to the Holy Spirit to lead you and command you with the divine authority to know and do God's will. Recognizin wrongful and pride-filled authority can help us destroy false gods and idols in our lives, so we can come to worship the living God in spirit and truth.

What About When I'm the Authority?

As far as exercisin authority in our own lives, Jesus revealed to us how He wants us to do that.

You may be sayin, "I don't have any authority over anybody!" If that's what you're sayin, don't be so sure. Maybe you do have authority over someone — a younger brother or sister, younger classmates in school, friends who look up to you, and people on the block or in your neighborhood who are watchin you like a hawk without you even knowin it!

Maybe you're in charge of somethin at school or in your parish — a club, sports team, or whatever! Regardless, you have authority over yourself!

This is critical, so open up the Scriptures and check out:

➡ Matthew 20:25-28

Followers of Christ exercise authority differently from others.

Notice that someone with "real" authority — the kind that comes from God above — exercises that authority a lot differently than someone who isn't sure that they really have any power. Real authority is exercised by servin — and I'm not talkin about tennis here!

R U servin or lordin it over those you have authority over in your life? Which also raises another question: How do I deal with legitimate authority? Do I see it as someone tryin to help me by servin me, or do I resent it, thinkin someone is just tryin to get over on me?

U Got 2 Believe — U Got 2 Trust

In order to get this authority thing, it's necessary to make a connection with the beautiful relationship between the grace of faith — that is, the ability to put my trust in God — and our ability to understand divine revelation, which flows from this faith. As St. Augustine said, "I believe in order to understand; and I understand, the better to believe."

Check this out:

Catechism of the Catholic Church ➡ #158

The Holy Spirit is always at work on our faith!

So you see that in order to understand all the awesome things that God has revealed through Jesus, Who has revealed these awesome things through the Church, U got 2 believe! U got 2 believe that Jesus has the authority to reveal, that He gave that authority to the Church, and that He will give you the authority to serve too! R U gettin it?

OK, So What's Been Revealed?

There are many key events of revelation in the Bible. One of them is what happened to Moses at the burnin bush. Moses was tendin the flock of his father-in-law Jethro. Moses came to Mount Horeb, the mountain of God, and there the angel of the Lord appeared to him in flames of fire from within a bush. He went to check it out and saw somethin really strange; the bush was up in flames but nothin was burnin up! Say what? Imagine? So what did Moses do?

Open up the Scriptures and check this out:

➡ Exodus 3

Yo, Moses! Take off your sandals before you enter here!

Maybe you've never seen anything like a burnin bush before — I haven't — but I'm sure you've had some kind of a strange experience that you did not understand, where God was speakin to you, revealin Himself. Don't worry. He could be settin you up like He set up Moses. Moses didn't panic, and everything cleared up for him. Don't panic — stay calm so you can pray.

The Bible tells us that the Lord would speak to Moses "face to face, as one speaks to a friend" (Exodus 33:11). That's what I'm talkin about. You see what a relationship with God is like? Two friends talkin to each other.

You might be thinkin, "I ain't no Moses. What about me?" Perhaps the thought of bein that close to God scares you. Don't you worry. Pray with this psalm: "Hear, O LORD, when I cry aloud, be gracious to me and answer me! 'Come,' my heart says, 'seek his face!' " (Psalm 27:7-8).

Be sure to check out the rest of Psalm 27; it's an awesome prayer. It will help you to keep your heart open to divine revelation, open to God speakin to your heart even through the strangest events of life.

The Big NOW!

Another cool thing about revelation is that it has a 3-D vibe, with a past, present, and future dimension. With God, it's all one. There's just one big "Now" that always was and always will be. But for us, in His love and mercy, God breaks out of that awesome Now to enable us to share in His life.

As we saw in Hebrews 1:1 "God spoke to our ancestors in many and various ways." He still speaks to us today, of course. Yet we know, as the Church teaches, that there will be "no further new public revelation before the glorious manifestation of our Lord Jesus Christ" (Dogmatic Constitution on Divine Revelation #4).

The Final Revelation

When Christ is gloriously manifested, there is goin to be a whole brand-new, big-time revelation that's gonna pull it all together. There will be good news and bad news. You can count on it! In Isaiah 40:5, we read, "Then the glory of the LORD shall be revealed, and all people shall see it together, for the mouth of the LORD has spoken."

St. Paul reminds us that we do not lack spiritual gifts necessary to recognize and accept the revelation of our Lord Jesus Christ. The problem is that we don't always use the spiritual gifts we have.

In 1 Corinthians 1:7-8, St. Paul tells us "you are not lacking in any spiritual gift as you wait for the revealing of our Lord Jesus Christ. He will also strengthen you to the end, so that you may be blameless on the day of our Lord Jesus Christ." If we rely on Jesus to keep us strong to the end, we'll be in good shape for some good news. If we don't rely on Jesus to keep us strong, we'll be in some serious trouble and get some really bad news.

Good News or Bad — It's Our Choice

Its kinda like the Last Judgment in Matthew 25.
Do you know it?

Open your Bible and read this:

➡ Matthew 25:31-46

When Jesus comes again in glory.

The good news is that if we stay faithful to Jesus, we'll be caught up in the glory of safe communion and union with the "whole crew": the Father, the Son, and the Holy Spirit; and all the saints in heaven. I'm really tryin to keep my heart and mind open to what God has said and is sayin, so that when it's all said and done, I'll hear Him say, "Enter into the joy of your master" (Matthew 25:21).

The bad news is that some folks might not make it. In Matthew 25:41, Jesus had some bad news for those who did not, would not, could not, or whatever, recognize the mystery of His hidden presence: "You that are accursed, depart from me into the eternal fire prepared for the devil and his angels."

So let's pray, pray, pray, and be really careful.

Findin God in Daily Life — Bein Found by God

The revelation of God doesn't just come to us in words, teachings, or sacraments. Along with these wonderful gifts of God to the Church, the revelation of God comes through ordinary difficult, and even ugly, experiences.

What am I talkin about? Being hungry, thirsty, alone, in need of clothes, being sick, and in prison. There's nothin pretty about people bein hungry, thirsty, alone, in need of clothing, sick, or in prison. Yet in some real and mysterious, awesome, and beautiful way, God reveals His presence. God comes to us!

Listen to Jesus! The reason for the bad news in Mathew 25:41 is given in verses 42 and 43. Did you read it yet?

These folks were kinda shocked when they heard the bad news. I'm sure they thought of themselves as good people, decent people that would do anything for Jesus if they knew He was in need. But hey, that's the point! Being a decent person is a good thing — but it's not enough!

We need to be in the truth, and as Catholics we've got the truth — the whole truth and nothin but the truth. The problem is that we don't always live it, and some of us don't live it because we don't know it. But God has revealed it! So time to get with it!

No Excuses — Get With It!

So get with it! Excuses and even so-called good excuses won't be of much help. These folks who got the bad news tried to wiggle out of it, but it didn't work. They kept repeatin, "Lord when did we see You? We saw the hungry, the naked, the sick, the imprisoned, but not You."

It's like they were sayin, "Boy, if I knew it was You, Lord, I really would have done things differently." Isn't it true? But ya know what? They didn't know it was Him. Don't let that happen to you! Lord, have mercy! Lord, spare us and open us up to the power of Your spirit and the mystery of Your presence!

I have a song on my CD Loved By You *called "Holy Masquerade." It's about how God comes to us in the mystery of a masquerade (that's a disguise), which can prevent us from recognizin the mystery of His presence. The song is really a prayer for the eye of our soul to see right. It's so easy for us to see wrongly — or worse still, not to see at all. It goes like this:*

As I walk the earth by day,
And pass away by night,
Bless the eye of my soul, help me see right.
Revelations of Your presence,
Pass by in this big parade,
The glory of Your holy masquerade.

You come to us, You show Yourself.
We do not realize,
The mystery of Your presence in disguise.
We miss You in Your lowliness,
And Your loftiness in the sky.
Your many faces, we sadly let pass by.

In every flower, in every tree,
In every place and face.
No matter how poor, how sick or how free.
Every day the splendor,
Of the sun passes on to fade,
The glory of Your holy masquerade.

Scripture, Tradition, creation, everyone, and everywhere are means by which God reveals His mystery, His love, and His presence. God reveals Himself in the best of times and worst of times — and even if and when we do recognize Him, we then tend to forget!

Don't Forget! Remember?

In the prophetic books of the Old Testament, we find God pleadin with His people to remember all that He had done for them. Over and over again, He has to remind His people about the revelation of His love. It's all about the basics! Did you ever watch *The Ten Commandments* on TV or see the video? And the people still don't get it? What's up with that? The Lord said, "I revealed myself to the family of your ancestor in Egypt when they were slaves to the house of Pharoah" (1 Samuel 2:27).

Not much has changed. They didn't get it then, and we ain't gettin it now. What are we waitin for? Lord, help us get it as You give it! Help us not to let You pass by as we strive to fulfill Your command to love one another as You have loved us.

The whole history of salvation from the first moment of creation is all about God revealin Himself and His people forgettin! Think about it. In Genesis, Chapter 2, God took Adam and put him in the garden and commanded him to take care of it. God also revealed to Adam the trouble he would be in if he ate from the tree of knowledge: ". . . for in the day that you eat of it you shall die" (Genesis 2:17).

"You shall die!" Think this promise of death made a difference? Adam even had the help of Eve, and both of them couldn't remember what God had revealed.

Oh yeah, Eve told the lyin Father of lies, who tried to trip her and Adam up, that "we may eat of the fruit of the trees in the garden; but God said, 'You shall not eat of the fruit of the tree that is in the middle of the garden, nor shall you touch it, or you shall die' " (Genesis 3:2-3).

Do the Right Thing!

I guess it goes to show that you can have all the right answers and still do the wrong thing! It ain't all about the right answers, even though the right answers are important.

It's all about God and bein loved and saved by Him — it's about bein faithful. So let's be careful! And be careful not to let the revelation of the Lord pass you by while you strive to be faithful to the Lord of the revelation!

Havin the fullness of the truth as Catholics is one thing — livin it is another thing! Yet, you really can't live it without havin it. Know what I'm sayin?

It's so easy to forget what God has revealed. That's why Jesus, when revealin the new and everlastin covenant on Holy Thursday, told us to "Do this in memory of me."

It's not enough just to receive divine revelation, to know God's love, mercy, and mystery. And it's not enough for us to know ourselves through Jesus. We must transmit that revelation, move it on from one person to another, cause it to spread like butter all over the bread — hand it on, pass it on.

Wretched man that I am! Who will rescue me from this body of death? Thanks be to God through Jesus Christ our Lord!

Romans 7:24-25

CHAPTER 3

Morality: Help!

No, No, No — HELP!

The title of this chapter on morality is "Morality: Help!"

This is what usually comes to mind when I hear the word *morality*. Moral laws, moral principals, regulations, rules, doing good, NO SEX, no this and no that. "No! No! No!" And if it matters — and it does (in fact, it is a matter of life and death) — then "Help! Help! Help!" is what comes to mind. Right?

Open your Bible up and check this out:

➡ Ephesians 5:5-10

St. Paul makes a list of those who won't make it into the kingdom of God.

In light of Ephesians 5:5-10 and not makin it into the Kingdom, this is serious stuff! No deception, no empty talk, havin to disassociate with certain people (not bein able to hang with certain people), havin to clean up your act, and bein concerned about the wrath of God. . . . Yo, I don't know about you, but somebody help me! Know what I'm sayin?

Immorality, impurity, and greed — the big three — are summed up by St. Paul into one as idolatry: That's number one, as in the First Commandment: "I am the LORD your God: you shall not have strange gods before me."

TIME OUT! While we're at it, let's get to all of them — you know, the "Big Ten":

1. I am the LORD your God: you shall not have strange gods before me.
2. You shall not take the name of the LORD your God in vain.
3. Remember to keep holy the LORD's Day.
4. Honor your father and your mother.
5. You shall not kill.
6. You shall not commit adultery.
7. You shall not steal.
8. You shall not bear false witness against your neighbor.
9. You shall not covet your neighbor's wife.
10. You shall not covet your neighbor's goods.

So What Is It?

What the heck is this morality thing anyway?

Let's check out Brother Webster to see what he says about morality:

Morality is a doctrine or system of moral conduct; particular moral principles of right human conduct; virtue.

Gettin into a topic is one thing. Gettin to the meaning of it is another thing. And gettin to the Person behind it all is the thing!

My own experience — and my experience of many young people and older people as well (the coolest and most authentic older people are really only young people who've been at it for a really long time) — is that morality means "No." Like I said, no this, no that, and NO SEX. That's it!

So "What you mean, Fadda?" "What's the point?"
Wrong question.

It's not all about a point. It's all about a Person: Jesus.

Not What, But Who

Jesus is the meaning behind all the stuff about morality. All those "no's" flow from a "yes" to Jesus. So if you ain't feelin the positive energy of those no's, maybe you're not feelin the awesome energy of a yes to Jesus. Maybe you never said that yes, or maybe you did say yes and need to say it one more time. So either way, whether you've never said yes to Jesus or if you've said yes a thousand times, say it again, even if you're sick of it because you keep fallin and failin.

My friend Father William McNamara likes to say, "It's the bounce that counts." It's true.

So let's pray before we go any further so we can keep bouncin back and not get discouraged. (Just in case you're really not ready for this prayer at this moment, skip over it for now, keep reading, and come back to it later.)

The "Yes to Jesus" Prayer

Lord Jesus, I accept You into my heart.
Forgive me my sins.
Heal my heart, mind, body, and soul
So I can follow You.
I give You permission to come to me
And to be the Lord of all of me,
Especially of those areas in my life where I struggle so
    much.
Set me free and on fire with the gift of Your love.
Amen!

One of the many things I really like about the *Catechism of the Catholic Church* with regard to the section on morality is that it's called "Life in Christ," and that's because it's all about Jesus. All the do's and don'ts are all about Jesus. So when we're not right with Him, it's no wonder we're havin a harder time than we need to have with all the morality stuff.

It's All About Jesus

No matter how you look at it, livin a moral life, a life in Christ, in the world today — especially for youth — is gonna be hard. But it doesn't have to be as hard as sometimes we make it.

In fact, you might be sayin, "What you mean 'hard,' Fadda? It's impossible!"

No kiddin! It might seem that way for sure. But remember, "For God all things are possible" (Matthew 19:26).

God has a taste for the impossible — He likes it. And if we stay close to Jesus, He will help us to acquire a taste for the impossible too. It's pretty cool!

Confusion

The first thing I want to point out is that there's so much confusion today. People are confused about what they think, confused about what they believe, confused about what they feel, and confused about how they make choices and behave. People are confused about what's right and what's wrong, and even confused about what's a sin and what's not a sin. It's all very confusing!

Check it out: I think confusion is one of the devil's most powerful tools. I know you know what confusion means, but it can't hurt to consult with Brother Webster one more time.

According to Brother Webster, confusion *means* to mix up, to embarrass, to disturb in mind or purpose, to make indistinct.

We can certainly see how "mixed-up" some people are today.

Confusion also means to make embarrassed. Have you ever done something stupid and really thought you were right, but found out the hard way that you were wrong? Kinda like goin to the pizza joint to pick up Friday night's dinner. Your family name is Murphy. You see "Murphy" on the pile of pizzas. You go to pick them up and start walkin toward the door to pay for them and the pizza man says those pizzas are for another set of Murphys. It's embarrassing.

Confusion also means to disturb in mind or purpose. This can get pretty deep. Have you ever been disturbed about whether you should break up with your boyfriend or girlfriend? Or been confused why your boyfriend or girlfriend broke up with you when all seemed to be goin well? It's very disturbing.

Confusion also means "to make indistinct." It's kinda like "shirts and skins" when you're runnin a full-court game of hoops in the park. In order to tell who's on whose team, one team keeps their shirts on (shirts) and the other team takes their shirts off (skins). Boys only, PLEASE!

TIME OUT! Most people know that sex before and outside of marriage is wrong. Lots of people disagree with that or have a difficult time dealin with that, and understandably so. But what blows me away is when I hear young people — very sincere young people, especially in confession — who really did not know that masturbation and oral sex were sins. So long as there's no goin "all the way" (technical word: intercourse; biblical word: fornication), then there's no sin. The only good thing about that was that these folks were really sincere and were really sorry. They confessed, repented, were forgiven, did penance, and bounced back really good! Alleluia!

Good or Evil?

This confusion between right and wrong, and good and evil, is really a big deal. One of my favorite spiritual writers, Rabbi Abraham Joshua Heschel, puts it this way in *Between God and Man*:

> The confusion of good and evil is the central problem of history and the ultimate issue of redemption. . . . All of history is a sphere where good is mixed with evil. The supreme task of man, his share in redeeming the work of creation, consists in an effort to separate good from evil, and evil from good.

Check out what the Second Vatican Council said:

For when the order of values is jumbled, and bad is mixed with the good, individuals and groups pay heed solely to their own interests, and not to those of others.

— *Pastoral Constitution on the Church in the Modern World #37*

Pope John Paul II was right on target, as usual, when he said, "In the confusion that reigns in the world today it is so easy to give in to illusion."

It's too easy! Remember, as Brother Webster points out, illusion is an erroneous, a wrong perception of reality or a wrong belief. It's so easy to be wrong and be confused in general, and especially with the faith. The really dangerous thing about it is that you might not even know that you're confused.

Blinded by the Wrong Light

All of this is rooted in the Bible. In 2 Corinthians 11:14, St. Paul tells us, "Even Satan disguises himself as an angel of light."

Also, in 2 Corinthians 4:4, Paul tells us that "the god of this world has blinded the minds of the unbelievers, to keep them from seeing the light of the gospel of the glory of Christ." If this can happen to unbelievers, you can be sure it can happen, did happen, does happen, will happen, and even is happenin to believers even as you're readin this! O Lord, do we need help — especially Your Help! See what I'm sayin?

Where It All Started

Why is it like this? Where did it come from? What does it mean? Well, thanks to that original sin thing, we all have this wound inside of us. As a result of this wound of original sin, we are inclined to evil and subject to error. We are divided in ourselves, all of us — all peoples, individuals, societies, and nations. There's so much struggle — and dramatic struggle at that — between good and evil, light and darkness.

Check this out:

Catechism of the Catholic Church   ➡ #1707

The struggle between good and evil is fierce.

It can get pretty intense. Our hearts are wounded. So you can now see why Jesus said in Mark 7:21-23, "For it is from within, from the human heart, that evil intentions come: fornication, theft, murder, adultery, avarice, wickedness, deceit, licentiousness, envy, slander, pride, folly. All these evil things come from within, and they defile a person."

That's why the Church teaches that the origin of all sin can be found within ourselves (check out CCC #1873). Got to be real careful here. It's only with God's help through the light of divine revelation that we can recognize sin clearly and not be tempted to excuse ourselves because of the way we were raised, some personal weakness, the bad social conditions we were exposed to as a child, etc.

The Church continues to teach us that it is only with an understanding of God's plan for us that "we grasp that sin is an abuse of the freedom that God gives to created persons so that they are capable of loving him and loving one another" (CCC #387).

Adam and Eve

Adam and Eve, the talkin snake, forgettin what God said, that one bite of the apple, and blamin and accusin each other really messed us all up.

Get your Bible and check this out:

➡ Genesis 3

The fall of humanity.

Then check this out:
Catechism of the Catholic Church ➡ #396-409

Thanks, Adam! Followin what the Bible says, the Church has always taught, and still does teach, that this mess that we are in and our inclination to choose evil can all be traced back to Adam's sin. (Check out CCC #403 again!) Did U read the *Catechism* yet? Get 2 it!

An Inclination Toward Evil

This inclination-toward-evil thing is what makes it all so intense.

An inclination is a natural disposition of mind or character. No wonder sin is so easy. In a certain sense, it's natural for us to sin. Check it out: An inclination is a tilting of somethin. Our "tilting," or inclination, to sin is gonna make it really hard for us to climb up the hill of doin God's will, the narrow road to heaven. Yet at the same time, it's gonna make it really easy for us to slide down the hill of the path to destruction. You don't have to do much to go rollin down that hill. Know what I'm sayin?

That's why Jesus commands us and teaches us to "enter through the narrow gate; for the gate is wide and the road is easy that leads to destruction, and there are many who take it. For the gate is narrow and the road is hard that leads to life, and there are few who find it" (Matthew 7:13-14).

The Zipper Zone

This wide gate and broad road that many enter which leads to destruction I call the "zipper zone." It's the way of our fallen nature, the way of our fallen flesh, and it's unfortunately celebrated by the culture of death.

On my Catholic rap CD Sacro Song, *which is dedicated to Pope John Paul II and the new evangelization, I have a song called "The Zipper Zone." The chorus is based on St. Paul's theology of the body:*

The body is the Lord's. Ya body is not your own.
The media has a bad plan, to drag you down to
    the zipper zone.

Check out the verses:

I.

They hit ya up hard on the radio,
Never stop talkin bout sex tryin to influence the way you
    go,
The words become pictures maliciously they show.
They want you to forget about the truth that you really
    know,
Deep down a child of God that's who you really are.
Next step to the TV store to get yourself a VCR,

Get cable get connected with more channels to select.
They wanna cast a spell on how ya choose and make a bad
　　effect.
Wake up, speak up, don't pretend protect a friend.
The bad plan of the media together we can end.
No more TV pollution into your holy home.
No more draggin you down to the zipper zone.

II.

The body is a gift from God it is good.
You could never praise and thank God enough even if ya
　　could.
I doubt if ya would,
The soul of the culture is defected.
Pro-choice pro-death so cruel life's not respected.
The sacredness of life and holy sex they neglect.
The mockery of family life
Reject it protect it
From prime time producers so slick and indirect.
The values of the nation they poison and misdirect.
Workin overtime on young people's intellect.
Be aware of what they're doin together we can correct.
The bad plan of the media together let's disown,
Yo no mo draggin us down to the zipper zone.

III.

They make ya burn with lust
Create an evil intention.
They say don't wait
Don't hesitate pursue ya sex direction.
Take the pill, wear a condom "play it safe just use protection."
It's all a big lie, you can still get AIDS infection.
What do you do? Play it safe HIV wait and see?
Life is precious life is short abstain and be free.
Save sex for marriage you can beat the disease.
Don't wait to fall on ya back to get down on ya knees.

> Thank God for your body, pray for self-control,
> Live according to God's will, achieve a higher goal.
> Listen up to what I'm sayin on the microphone,
> No more draggin you down to the zipper zone.

So the whole thing is really messed up. I don't think I have to convince you of that. No need here to be specific about namin schools, families, cities, countries, churches, friends, strangers, etc., to prove the point. Your own experience — especially with the "help" of the media's fascination with what's wrong and with the glamour of evil — is more than enough.

The Bible teaches us that "the whole world lies under the power of the evil one" (1 John 5:19), and that "like a roaring lion your adversary the devil prowls around, looking for someone to devour" (1 Peter 5:8).

So to be sober and vigilant, resistin the evil one, solid in our faith in Jesus Christ and His Church, is goin to be a battle. It's all a big battle.

Check this out:

Catechism of the Catholic Church ➡ #409

The history of humanity has been a constant struggle. We need God's grace!

It all sounds kinda grim — so negative and fierce and gloomy. What's the point of all this stuff, especially if this is just the beginnin? What about this life-in-Christ thing? What's morality got to do with Jesus and me followin Him?

Conversion — Turnin Our Lives Around Toward Jesus

Before we go any further, we have to come to the bottom line of all this morality stuff: Jesus. What does it mean every day for you and me 24/7 (twenty-four hours a day, seven days a week)? It means conversion — constantly turnin to Jesus.

The best definition of conversion I have ever heard comes from Pope John Paul II — who I affectionately and lovingly call "JP." He's my hero!

If you get nothin else from this chapter, or if you get nothin else from this book, GET THIS — Pope John Paul II's definition of conversion:

[Conversion] gives rise to a dynamic and lifelong process which demands a continual turning away from "life according to the flesh" to "life according to the Spirit" (cf. Rom 8:3-13). Conversion means accepting, by a personal decision, the saving sovereignty of Christ and becoming his disciple.

— The Mission of the Redeemer #46

See what he's sayin? See what I'm sayin? Are you gettin it yet? This sin and morality stuff can get you down? Amen? But Jesus wants to raise us up again and again, and forever and ever, amen! Again and again the same sins and struggles right? Sound familiar?

No Condemnation for Those in Christ Jesus

I've been at this conversion thing for a good long while. Getting close to 25 years! I have to tell ya, it gets better every day, and it's worth it. It's so very worth it.

Yet, I hear lots of young people and old people all over the country and all over the world sayin the same thing: "I'm sick and tired of this sin thing. I can't do anything about it, so why bother? What the heck — might as well sin and get it over with."

Did you ever feel like that?

Sometimes people feel condemned by God and condemned by others and even condemned by themselves! That's not cool. I'm sure we all can click with St. Paul on this one: "Wretched man that I am! Who will rescue me from this body of death? Thanks be to God through Jesus Christ our Lord!" (Romans 7:24-25).

If you really wana go deeper into this, read and re-read all of these two chapters:

➥ Romans 7 and 8

Check out what St. Paul says about condemnation.

Did you read it? Then you now know that there is no condemnation for those who are in Christ Jesus. Right?

Be careful not to get caught up in the negative thing and identify that as what a relationship with Jesus and His Church is all about. Jesus and the Church are all about a big YES! Sayin yes to Jesus and His Spirit opens the door for a new life where we find ourselves livin in conformity to God's plan.

The Bible tells us that there is a law of the spirit of life in Christ Jesus. This is the morality thing in a nutshell! It's connected to and flows from Jesus and life in His Spirit. Say yes to Jesus and you'll see what I'm talkin bout!

What Are U Really Concerned About?

What are you concerned with? Good question, hey? What and who do you relate to? Who do you hang with, and who do you really want to hang with? Who and what influence you? Who and what are you involved with? Who and what occupy your mind?

These questions kinda remind me of a woodcarving I once saw. It's a little gross, but it's a good and honest reflection of the struggle.

The carving was of a monk. His head was bowed in a prayerful posture, and half of his head was carved in the shape of a beautiful naked body part of a beautiful woman! See what I'm sayin? That's what was almost a 24/7 concern of his. I'm sure it was unwanted, but it was there! I can testify to this, especially as a celibate — as a man who has followed the Gospel call to renounce marriage and sex for the sake of the Kingdom.

It's not easy. I'm not only talkin about the celibate thing but the whole morality thing. In fact, it's really hard. As a matter of fact, it's impossible! But remember what I said earlier: With man, it's impossible; but with God, all things are possible! Life in Christ, in the power of His Holy Spirit, is an awesome adventure to say the least!

Things of the Flesh

Y'all are watchin MTV and other shows like it and worse. These shows are concerned with the things of the flesh, and by you watchin them you become concerned with the things of the flesh. It's hard enough all on your own not to get all caught up in that stuff, so don't let them help you go the wrong way! Even lots of the music you listen to is concerned with the flesh.

There's "The Jerry Springer Show." I regret even mentionin it! But lots of y'all are watchin it and shows like it! These shows give a false sense of being concerned about people's lives. Are they really concerned? The truth is no — and the truth will set you free! Why doesn't Jerry ever put members of his family on that show to "help" them? He probably would never do it! These kinda shows are concerned with the things of the flesh. As goes the show, so goes those who watch it!

Pluses and Minuses

Let's make somethin perfectly clear here. The flesh is good.

Remember, "the word became flesh" (John 1:14), which means that God took on our human flesh. It's a blessed and positive thing.

There's also a negative dimension because of sin. In order for you not to be confused, the things of "the flesh" have been listed in the Bible in a number of different places.

Let's check out St. Paul in Galatians 5:19-21. The following list is the exact order from the Bible:

(1) Fornication, (2) Impurity, (3) Licentiousness, (4) Idolatry, (5) Sorcery, (6) Enmities, (7) Strife, (8), Jealousy, (9) Anger, (10) Quarrels, (11) Dissensions, (12) Factions, (13) Envy, (14) Drunkenness, (15) Carousing, and (16) "things like these. . . ."

Doesn't it sound like a description of "The Jerry Springer Show"?

Warning!

You've read the list from St. Paul. Now read what he says in conclusion. He concludes with a warnin. He says:

> I am warning you, as I warned you before: those who do such things will not inherit the kingdom of God. (Galatians 5:21)

Don't get me wrong. I ain't sayin Jerry Springer ain't gettin into the Kingdom. But he sure ain't helpin us and the many, many people who unfortunately watch his show.

Regarding the media, our Holy Father said that they must make it their concern to make themselves witnesses to the truth "so that the human person will always be respected" (Address to Journalists, June 4, 2000).

Wouldn't it be great if they really and truly respected people on the show?

I can't judge Jerry Springer or anybody else. I've got enough to worry about in my own life. Yet, at the same time, I hope that his show and others like it will utilize their full potential for good and stop celebratin the pain and sins of our people! Life can be hard, and Jesus knows what's up. Jesus needs no one to testify to what's goin on in our fallen human nature.

What Do U Treasure?

It all boils down to what we choose, and what we choose is intensely influenced by what we treasure. That's another way of talkin about what concerns us.

It's so easy to be concerned with the things of the flesh, right?

1. **Materialism:** I am what I possess. And if I can't get what I want, I'm nothin, I have no value as a person. The more I have, the better I am. *No!*

2. **Secularism:** I can pull this life thing off all by myself. I can do it on my own. I don't need to believe in God or nobody else. *Not true!*

3. **Sensuality:** As long as it feels good and looks good, it's up for grabs. I don't have to wait until I'm married to have sex or for anythin else. As long as I look good and feel good, it's all good. The glamour of TV and advertising. *Wrong!*

Concupi . . . What?

All of this is part of the "tilt" thing, the inclination toward evil I spoke about earlier.

Our Tradition calls it "concupiscence." This ugly thing stays with us, the Church teaches, so that with the help of the grace of Christ we may prove ourselves in the struggle of Christian life (check out CCC #1426).

Jesus put it this way: "For where your treasure is, there your heart will be also" (Luke 12:34). A treasure is somethin of great wealth or value, somethin we cherish or really appreciate. In other words, somethin or someone we concern ourselves with, maybe even with all our heart, even to a fault.

Where's Your Heart?

What's your treasure? Think about some of the things or relationships you really value that might not be and probably are not good for you: too much sugar, too much boyfriend or girlfriend; too much alcohol, music, sports, computer, Internet, videos and video/computer games; illegal use of drugs (even if it's "just smoking pot," weed, reefer, blunt, or whatever you might call it); sexual activity with yourself (masturbation — check out CCC #2352) or with someone else, even if it's not fornication or adultery.

It's easy to be very concerned about these things, for them to be a kind of treasure. Even if it's "just a little bit," there will your heart be *just a little bit*. With some of this stuff that can be so powerful, a little bit is already a little too much. Believe it. It could and does happen.

This heart of ours is tricky business. It's certainly a blessin, but our heart can certainly be a burden too. The burden and the blessin of the heart is not unfamiliar territory to Jesus. In fact, He is very familiar with this dimension of life. That's why Jesus said, "Come to me, all you that are weary and are carrying heavy burdens, and I will give you rest. Take my yoke upon you, and learn from me; for I am gentle and humble in heart, and you will find rest for your souls. For my yoke is easy, and my burden is light" (Matthew 11:28-30).

St. Augustine — Great Sinners Can Make Great Saints!

The heart, the heart, the heart!

I think of the great St. Augustine, a man of great heart and great passion. Did you ever see a statue of him holdin a heart? I love him — he's all passion!

Augustine was a great sinner and became an even greater saint. Oh yeah! He lived with great passion as a sinner. He had at least one child out of wedlock, and that child was not obtained through an adoption agency — know what I'm sayin? Augustine made da baby!

TIME OUT! Adoption is a great option for folks who can't have their own kids or if someone gets pregnant and feels she can't keep the baby. Don't fall for the lie of the abortion solution. It's a legal and tragic sin. As one of my favorite bumper stickers says, "Abortion: One Dead — One Wounded." (By the way, if you ever had an abortion or helped someone have one, God can deal with that — repent, go to confession and get forgiven, and begin the long healing process.)

St. Augustine prayed with great passion. Early on he prayed, "Lord make me chaste [give me self-control over my sexuality] but not yet." Got to love him!

St. Augustine also lived his life in Christ with great passion and became a great saint. That's the point of it all for all of us! He prayed, "You have made us for Yourself, O God, and our hearts are restless until they rest in You."

I was so deeply moved by St. Augustine's passion and prayer that I wound up singin it, puttin it to music, and recordin it. It's called "The Prayer of St. Augustine." It's on my First Collection CD. Check it out:

Oh beauty so ancient and yet so new,
Too late have I known You, too late have I loved You.
For behold, You were within me and I was outside,
And in an ugly way, I cast myself
On the beautiful things of creation, which are beautiful
    cause You made them.

La la la la la la la la la la

For You were with me but I was not with You
But You shouted out and cast away my deafness.
You burned bright before me and broke through my
    blindness.
You breathed Your fragrances upon me
And even now do I pant after Thee.

La la la la la la la la la la

You touched me and I burned for Your peace,
O Lord.
For You have made us for Yourself, O God.
And our hearts are restless until they rest in You.
Too late have I known You, too late have I loved You.

O Jesus Christ, my Lord and my Redeemer,
From what dark place did You call my will.
And now I am prepared to do those things of which I was
    afraid.
And now I'm not afraid to surrender those things which I
    once found so pleasing.

La la la la la la la la la

For You have come and You have taken their place,
You who are brighter than all brightness.
But not to those who look into the darkness,
You who are deeper than all mystery.
But not to those who are proud unto themselves.

La la la la la la la la la

O Lord, You came and took the place of all my desire,
You who are my goodness and my hope.
My fulfillment, my salvation, my happiness.
Too late have I known You, too late have I loved You.
My expectation, my love of my friends and neighbors, my
    hope, my joy, my fulfillment,
My salvation, my Lord, my God, and my All.

You touched me and I burned for Your peace, O Lord.
For You have made us for Yourself, O God. And our hearts
    are restless until they rest in You.
Too late have I known You, too late have I loved You.

The life of St. Augustine shows us that the passions are in themselves neither good or evil. When the passion of love was influenced by the vice of lust and the sin of selfishness, Augustine was moved to sin and have sex outside of marriage. He messed up big time. Yet when this same passion — love — was influenced by the Holy Spirit, Augustine used all his God-given gifts and talents for the Lord, and he was inspired and empowered by the Holy Spirit to become a great saint.

Passion

What exactly are we talkin about anyway?

Brother Webster tells us that the word passion *can mean:*

- A powerful emotion, like love or anger.
- A strong sexual desire, like lust.
- The Passion, or suffering, of Jesus.
- Boundless enthusiasm, like passion for sports.

The Church teaches us that the passions are "emotions or movements of the sensitive appetite that incline us to act or not to act in regard to something felt or imagined to be good or evil" (CCC #1763). In other words, our actions are influenced by these passions — feelings, emotions, or movements — within our hearts that get us fired up, pumped up, in a good way or in a bad way.

The Big 7

There are seven principal passions: (1) love, (2) hatred, (3) desire, (4) fear, (5) joy, (6) sadness, and (7) anger.

You might be askin, "How can anger or hatred be good?" If I was the coach of your basketball team, I want you to hate loosin and to be angry when you do lose a game! It's an anger and a hatred you'll get over, and it will motivate you to a deeper commitment to do the necessary things for us to win.

After all, I hate my sins. I get angry at myself when I do sin. See what I'm sayin? By God's grace and a good confession, I bounce back and strive to deepen my commitment to Jesus.

Check out JP's definition of passion: " 'Passion' means a passionate love, unconditioned self-giving: Christ's passion is the summit of an entire life 'given' to his brothers and sisters to reveal the heart of the Father" (from Pope John Paul II's message for the Fifteenth World Youth Day). From this revelation of the heart of the Father flows the energy that helps us keep on believin. U got 2 believe!

OK, so this passion thing you might agree is cool and could even be somewhat helpful. But how do you know? How do you know when the passions are bein dragged down by the vices or bein lifted up by the virtues? What if I like my virtues to be vices, or vice-a-versa?

It can all be a bit confusing. Just in case this is what you're feelin or thinkin, remember what I said about confusion.

There's another word we have to check out, and that's *conscience*. How do I know when I'm livin my life in Christ?

How Do I Know If I'm Livin in Christ?

Isn't conscience what enables me to do what I want, like "Well, according to my conscience, sleepin with my girlfriend (or boyfriend) doesn't really bother me because there's true and mutual love between us"? No, that's not conscience.

What about "Well, I skipped Mass this past Sunday and that's OK"? No, that's not it either. It's not OK to miss Mass, and this is not conscience. Missin Mass on Sunday is a sin and needs to be confessed.

Well, then, what is conscience?

First of all, the Church teaches us that conscience is that voice within us that we must obey. This voice that we must obey ain't my voice or your voice. It's God's voice. That's pretty deep, and even that can be confusing. So you might be sayin, "Hold on. If it's not my voice but God's voice and I must obey it, how the heck do I know the difference? How do I know when it's God's voice or my voice?" Good question. Let's take it one step at a time.

Read this:

Catechism of the Catholic Church ➡ #1776

The Church teaches that there is law within us that we must obey.

Conscience

I'm sure you've felt the effects of that voice echoing inside you, especially when you're about to do somethin wrong: "No, don't do it." That's your conscience, not just your fear of gettin caught. Takin money from your mom or dad's extra cash flow, underage purchasin and drinkin of alcohol, first time flirts with drugs, or sexual experiments. "Don't do it."

Have you ever been drivin on the highway and seen a person fixin a flat: "Stop and help." Ever see a homeless person in the street and hear the voice say, "Go and get him somethin to eat." That's your conscience at work.

Cardinal John Henry Newman said somethin really cool about this. He called conscience the "aboriginal Vicar of Christ." The word *aboriginal* here means first, or earliest of its kind. Conscience is the earliest Vicar of Christ, tellin us what to do and what to avoid. It's the inner voice of God's authority, directin us to live life in Christ Jesus.

So this conscience thing puts some responsibility on us. We have to listen — somethin we may not be very good at because we're not used to it. We have to get used to listenin. This could be a problem for most of us. We're so used to talkin and bein talked at. O Lord, help us to listen. Learnin how to listen will enable us to hear the voice of our conscience. Hearin is the key to obeyin. There you have it!

We have to make prudent judgments, judgments made with discipline and the good use of reason. Basically, we have to become responsible for our actions. One of the greatest responsibilities will be the correct formation of our conscience. The Church teaches that a correctly formed conscience will make judgments "according to reason, in conformity with the true good willed by the wisdom of the Creator" (CCC #1783).

Formation of Conscience

The good news here is that this education of our conscience is a "lifelong task" — so your conscience and your correct formation of it, listenin to it, and obeyin it will definitely keep you busy! It is important and beneficial to have a "good" conscience. Make sure you check out some of the benefits.

Read this:

Catechism of the Catholic Church ➡ #1784

*The Church spells out the benefits of a good
conscience, including peace of heart!*

Yes, yes, yes! Peace of heart! Lord, give us some of that sweet peace of heart.

Amen?

Jesus has overcome the world. How can I overcome myself and listen to the voice of God echoin in my conscience and correctly form my conscience?

On the one hand, it's easy. On the other hand, it's not so easy. So we have to put the two hands together and pray.

The light for the correct formation of our conscience comes from the Word of God and the teaching of the Church. The Church teaches us that we must make the Word of God our own, by what we believe, by how we pray, and finally by how we act (check out CCC #1785).

To assimilate the Word of God means to absorb it into our system — to read the Scriptures, especially the Gospels, so they get absorbed into our system of thinkin, feelin, and behavin. As this begins to happen, we will be able to give the Holy Spirit permission to work more powerfully in our lives so that we can live our lives in Christ.

Our Helper — the Holy Spirit

Jesus said He would send the Holy Spirit to us: "And when he comes, he will prove the world wrong about sin" (John 16:8). This means that the Holy Spirit will show us and convince us of when we are doin wrong and sinnin. This produces good and godly guilt, which leads to repentance, which leads to authentic freedom.

This is very different from bad worldly guilt that the devil uses to keep us in the bondage of shame. Rather than feelin guilty for a wrong act we may have done, and then repentin, confessin, doin penance, gettin over it and gettin on with our life, we feel shame about who we are, regret that we even are alive, and render ourselves unlovable by God or anybody else, especially ourselves.

St. Paul puts it this way: "For godly grief produces a repentance that leads to salvation and brings no regret, but worldly grief produces death" (2 Corinthians 7:10).

It's crucial that we know Jesus personally and that He "has authority on earth to forgive sins" (Matthew 9:6).

It's only in God through Jesus that "we have redemption through his blood, the forgiveness of trespasses, according to the riches of his grace that he lavished on us" (Ephesians 1:7-8).

So in light of all this, it's important to know that this sin thing really messes us up! The Church teaches that sin is an offense against God, and it is an act whereby we place ourselves against God, turning our backs on His love and will for us (check out CCC #1850).

Sin also "wounds the nature of man and injures human solidarity" (CCC #1849). In other words, it messes up everyone's life, not just ours!

Types of Sin

We need to say a word about the different kinds of sin, venial and mortal.

The Bible tells us that "all wrongdoing is sin, but there is sin that is not mortal" (1 John 5:17). The Church calls these sins "venial sins."

An uncharitable thought or word, an act of kindness or charity left undone — like offerin to help do the dishes without being asked, or cleanin up your room, or helpin a friend or neighbor. The word *venial* simply means excusable. These are sins that do not lead to death, even though they are wrong and need to be forgiven.

Acts of charity can wipe away venial sins (check out CCC #1394).

There are, however, deadly, or mortal, sins. If somethin is mortal, it causes death and is marked by great severity and intensity. Real serious here. That's why the Bible and the Tradition of the Church warn about sins that lead to death. We call these sins "mortal sins." There are three conditions that together must be met for a sin to be mortal.

Check it out:

Catechism of the Catholic Church ➥ #1854-1864

The three conditions for a sin to be mortal:
1. It must be a grave, or serious, matter. *Any breaking of the Ten Commandments is a serious matter. Some may be more serious that others. Murder is more serious than stealin.*
2. It must be committed with full knowledge. *This means that you really know, fully, that what you are doin is wrong.*
3. It must be committed with complete consent. *This means that you completely give permission and are in complete agreement and approve to freely commit the serious act you know to be wrong.*

All these conditions must be present in order for a sin to be mortal. In light of all this, it's important to remember that the Church teaches that "the promptings of feelings and passions can also diminish the voluntary and free character of the offense, as can external pressures or pathological disorders" (CCC #1860). This is good to keep in mind. Thanks be to God!

Need for Confession!

These deadly sins must be brought to confession. Our own prayer cannot handle these sins — they're deadly. Nothin to fear, though. We need repentance, and the power of God's forgiveness that comes to us through the saving passion, death, and resurrection of Jesus and the authority He gave to His Church. C Y U got 2 believe? Amen!

Jesus said to His apostles, "If you forgive the sins of any, they are fogiven them; if you retain the sins of any, they are retained" (John 20:23). Amen!

Here goes the biggie:

> "And I tell you, you are Peter, and on this rock I will build my church, and the gates of Hades will not prevail against it. I will give you the keys of the kingdom of heaven, and whatever you bind on earth will be bound in heaven, and whatever you loose on earth will be loosed in heaven." (Matthew 16:18-19)

If you want to stay close to Jesus, if you want to live a life in Christ — a life of charity, confoundin the confusion with the power of a correctly formed conscience — then confession and contrition are the keys to the joy that flows from the love and mercy that bring us forgiveness, healin, and salvation.

There is nothin to fear, and everythin to gain. It's all ours!

TIME OUT! Rabbi Abraham Heschel, one of my favorite spiritual writers, beautifully shows us how contrition is the path to follow the call to perfection, the call to love, our vocation to live the divine life. Check out what he says in God in Search of Man:

Comforting as the reliance upon moments of pure devotion is, the anxiety remains. After all our efforts and attempts to purify the self, we discover that envy, vanity, pride continue to prowl in the dark. Whence cometh our help? The moments of ecstatic self-forgetfulness pass quickly. What then is the answer?

Should we then despair because of our being unable to retain perfect purity? We should if perfection were our goal. However, we are not obliged to be perfect once and for all, but only to rise again and again beyond the level of self. Perfection is divine and to make it a goal of man is to call man to be divine. All we can do is to try to wring our hearts clean in contrition. Contrition begins with a feeling of shame at our being incapable of disentanglement from self. To be contrite at our failures is holier than to be complacent in perfection.

That's why Jesus instituted the sacraments, and that's why the Church hands them down to us to enliven us with divine life and to help us on our daily journey. We'll look at them more closely in the next chapter. U got 2 believe!

His divine power has given us everything needed for life and godliness, through the knowledge of him who called us by his own glory and goodness.

2 Peter 1:3

CHAPTER 4

Sacraments: Divine Power

More Stuff I Have to Do?

Sacraments!

When you hear that word, what's the first thing that comes to your mind?

Maybe something like "Ever since I made my first Holy Communion I 'have to' go to Mass every Sunday."

Or maybe "I can't wait for these dumb confirmation classes to get over with so I can be all finished with the 'Church thing.' "

And you probably don't even remember your baptism.

So that's three of the seven you've probably experienced, leavin four more to go! I know you probably know that there are seven sacraments, right?

Check it out:

1. Baptism
2. Confirmation
3. Eucharist

And don't forget about

4. Penance (Reconciliation)

Most folks wanna forget about that one! Who wants to tell some priest their sins?

So there's four. Which leaves us with

5. Matrimony
6. Holy Orders
7. Anointing of the Sick

Now, you might be sayin, "So what the heck is the big deal?" Like I've been sayin all along, if you don't know Jesus by experience, and just know about Him, there ain't gonna be no big deal because Jesus Himself is the Big Deal!

Stop right here and check out:

 2 Peter 1:3-8

In these passages, Peter talks about God giving us the awesome ability to share in the divine life.

Devotion

Do you see what the Word of God in 2 Peter is sayin about a life of devotion? Did you read it yet?

Let me tell you somethin: You can't have a life of devotion without first havin a relationship with Jesus.

If you check out the word devotion with Brother Webster, you'll see that it means religious fervor, an act of prayer or worship; the state of being ardently dedicated and loyal to an idea or a person.

There's a lot bein said right here — check it out.

We're talkin about religious fervor.

I'll bet you know what fervor is. It's an intensity of feeling or expression.

Fervor is like cheerin or booin at a basketball game or some other sporting event.

Fervor also means intense heat. So another way of puttin it is "bein fired up" — in this case, fired up for Jesus! We're also talkin about bein ardently devoted to a person or an idea. Jesus is a person, a divine Person with a divine nature and a human nature. We're talkin about bein ardently devoted to Him.

This means that our relationship with Jesus can't just be a nice little head-trip with some idea!

Don't get me wrong; it's too easy to get off on a head-trip with Jesus and many other things. Hopefully, our relationship with Jesus will be characterized by, as Brother Webster puts it, warmth of feeling expressed in eager, zealous support and activity. In other words, we will be alive in Christ.

That's what the sacraments are all about!

Fire From Heaven

Remember what happened on the day of Pentecost?

The Bible tells us, "Divided tongues, as of fire, appeared among them, and a tongue rested on each of them" (Acts 2:3).

The Holy Spirit actually came upon them!

All of those present — the apostles and our Blessed Mother — all literally got fired up and started goin out to the whole world to tell everyone about Jesus.

Some of them really paid for it — and I don't mean with cash, but with their blood.

I happen to be in Rome as I'm writin this chapter. It's pretty awesome!

Rome is the place where St. Peter and St. Paul shed their blood for Jesus, because He shed His blood for them. Now that's the ultimate expression of a life of devotion! Do you see where this is goin? Are you feelin me?

Now we're gettin ready to talk about the sacraments, and hopefully this will help you to start livin them, to keep livin them, or maybe to make a new beginning if you've fallen away — to help you shine more brightly with the light of Christ.

A Gift From Jesus

The sacraments were given to us by Jesus to help us live a life of devotion so that through knowledge of Him, who called us by His own glory and power, we may come to share in His divine nature. Remember what 2 Peter said? Have you read it yet? C'mon.

This is how we live out the mystery of our salvation in Christ. Here's how it works:

- Three get us into Christ, the sacraments of initiation: baptism, Eucharist, and confirmation.
- Two more are for our healing in Christ: penance (reconciliation) and the anointing of the sick.
- The last two are for the service of communion with Christ: holy orders and matrimony.

The whole point of the sacraments is to keep us alive in Jesus now and forever!

Listen to Some Experts

St Thomas Aquinas, a Doctor of the Church (a title for someone noted for his or her outstanding teaching), said, "The riches of Christ are communicated . . . through the sacraments."

The Church teaches that the sacraments are " 'powers that come forth' from the Body of Christ, which is ever-living and life-giving. They are actions of the Holy Spirit at work in his Body, the Church. They are 'the masterworks of God' in the new and everlasting covenant" (CCC #1116).

St. Augustine goes so far as to say that "the sacraments make the Church" because they communicate to us the mystery of communion with God, especially in the Eucharist. They provide divine protection for our vocation to divine worship and to serve the Church (check out CCC #1121).

The effect of sacramental life is that we literally become "partakers in the divine nature" by being united with God (check out CCC #1129).

The sacraments "confer the grace that they signify." They give us grace (check out CCC #1127).

The purpose of the sacraments is to sanctify, to make us holy, and to build up the Body of Christ, as well as to give worship to God and instruct the worshipers. Remember, Jesus told us that the Father seeks those who worship in spirit and truth, "for the Father seeks such as these to worship him" (John 4:23).

That's how awesome our sacraments are. They make us and keep us as the kind of worshipers our heavenly Father seeks. Is that you?

If This Is True, Why Am I Bored?

If it's true that the sacraments are "powers," and it is true, than how can it be that so many people experience the sacraments as "boring"?

The answer is simple: "The fruits of the sacraments also depend on the disposition of the one who receives them" (CCC #1128). The Church is tellin us that our disposition has a key role to play if the sacraments are to be happenin in our lives, makin us worshipers in spirit and truth.

This disposition thing is huge.

Check it out:
Among other things, disposition *is* the act or power of disposing. To dispose means to set in readiness. *That's awesome! To be ready every time we go to the sacraments.*

Your readiness is necessary for the sacraments to be fruitful in your life. This takes the blame off others and calls us to be responsible, to be ready.

Are You Ready for. . . ?

Jesus talks a lot about being ready.

Check this out:

➥ Matthew 22:1-14

The Parable of the Wedding Banquet.
Notice all the excuses?

Everybody that was invited to the wedding banquet had somethin else that was "important to do." They weren't ready.

Jesus concludes by sayin "many are called, but few are chosen" (Matthew 22:14). Stop right here.

Read this:

➡ Matthew 24:36-44

Jesus teaches us about the need to be ready.

Did you read what Jesus says about the need to be ready? He says that "you also must be ready, for the Son of Man is coming at an unexpected hour" (Matthew 24:44). Make sure you take a look in your Bible!

If you need more convincin, check out the wise and foolish virgins in Matthew 25:1-13. Also look at Luke 12:35-40.

Make Sure You're Ready

Before we get into the individual sacraments, the bottom line here is to make a connection between sacraments and bein ready. You can complain if you want about what's not happenin in your parish, or you can get yourself and your friends ready and make somethin happen. Know what I'm sayin? Make a connection in such a way that you actually do somethin about it. At least do somethin to prepare yourself for Mass and confession. This will help the power and graces of all the other sacraments to kick in! What's goin on or not goin on in our lives is gonna make a big difference on what kind of experience we have with the sacraments.

Think about it. Isn't it true with sports? You can have the greatest coach and be on a great team, but if you ain't in shape physically and mentally, and if you're not ready to give it your all, your experience with the team and in the game will not be what it could be. You will not be happenin that day. You will not be fruitful. Your teammates might carry you, but that won't happen forever. Havin a bad day, or fallin into a slump, is one thing. But not tryin and not bein ready is another thing. It's unacceptable and inexcusable. You "wit" me on that?

Most people are uninvolved and frustrated with the sacraments. They're frustrated because they're uninvolved. They're uninvolved because they're not ready. Time to wake up, y'all!

If you say that "church is borin," and you feel that "there ain't nothin happenin" with the sacraments, chances are there ain't nothin happenin in your preparation for the sacraments.

When was the last time — if ever — you read the Scripture readings for Mass before you went to Mass? See what I'm sayin?

- Do you even know how to find out what the readings are?
- Do you have a Sunday or weekday missal (that's a special book that has all the Scripture readings and all the prayers for Mass plus more)?
- Have you ever tried to take the readings as they're listed in the missal booklet in church and look up the readings in your Bible?
- Do you even have your own Bible? Have you ever talked about the readings with a family member or a friend? They'll probable think you're crazy, right?
- Have you ever not received Communion because you realized you committed a serious sin and didn't have the chance to go to confession?

These are all part of the disposition thing of bein ready, of preparin the way for an awesome experience with the Lord every time we participate in the Mass.

I like to put it this way: The level of your celebration depends on the level of your preparation. This is true for everything in life, and especially for the sacraments.

St. Paul said that we must "examine ourselves," make sure our disposition is in a good place. He said we should be sure we're ready. There are consequences:

For all who eat and drink without discerning the body, eat and drink judgment against themselves. For this reason many of you are weak and ill, and some have died. But if we judged ourselves, we would not be judged. (1 Corinthians 11:29-31)

If You Ain't Readin, You Won't Be Feedin!

The questions I just asked about whether you read the Scriptures before you go to Mass is a big one. I don't know if you know this, but the Catholic Church has always treated the Word of God (the Scriptures — the Bible) as she does the very Body of Christ. The Eucharist, the Bread of Life, is given "from the one table of God's Word and Christ's Body" (CCC #103).

The point is that there's a huge connection between the Word of God and the sacraments. The sacraments draw their nourishment from the Word of God. U got 2 believe! Know what I'm sayin?

It's so crucial for Catholics to read the Word of God in order to experience the power of the sacraments. The Church teaches that the sacraments cannot be celebrated without the proclamation of the Word of God, which presents to us the faith by which the sacraments naturally flow (check out CCC #1122).

Remember, the sacraments are actions of the Holy Spirit, and at the same time the Holy Spirit gives us "a spiritual understanding of the Word of God" (check out CCC #1101). The spiritual understanding of the Word of God through the power of the Holy Spirit keeps us in a living relationship with Jesus through the very structure and celebration of the sacraments.

So if you ain't readin, you won't be feedin on the power present and available in the sacraments.

Sacraments Are Rooted in Creation

Another cool thing about the sacraments is that they are signs rooted in the work of creation and human culture.

Water, bread, wine, oil — sounds like a meal! That's the point! It's somethin everybody can relate to, and these signs were taken up by Jesus and transformed by Him!

This is supposed to help us make and deepen the connection between the supernatural life and our daily life so we can see that God desires for us to share in the divine nature.

Pope St. Leo the Great said, "What was visible in our Savior has passed over into his mysteries" — that is, His sacraments. The sacraments are signs that our human nature can understand, and they make real and effective the grace they signify. There's a really important word used a lot with the sacraments: *efficacious*.

If something is efficacious *that means* it has the power to produce a desired effect.

The sacraments "make present efficaciously the grace that they signify" (CCC #1084).

Liturgy

All of the sacraments are celebrated in what is called the liturgy of the Church. You could think of the liturgy as "Church stuff."

The word liturgy *means* public service or work on behalf of the people.

For us, liturgy is the "participation of the People of God in 'the work of God' " (CCC #1069). This work of God was the main focus of Jesus when He walked the earth. In John 17:4, Jesus said to the Father, " I glorified you on earth by finishing the work that you gave me to do."

This is the Church's liturgy, celebratin and sharin in the work the Father gave Jesus to do. Liturgy is the work of Christ and the action of His Church (check out CCC #1071). It's the celebration of the Christian mysteries.

This work is the great mystery of the Father's will done perfectly in Jesus Christ — Christ crucified. Check out the beautiful teaching of St. Augustine, who said, "It was from the side of Christ as he slept the sleep of death upon the cross that there came forth the wondrous sacraments of the Church."

This is called the *Pascal Mystery*, the event by which Jesus accomplished the work of our salvation. "It is this mystery of Christ that the Church proclaims and celebrates in her liturgy so that the faithful may live from it and bear witness to it in the world" (CCC #1068).

The Paschal Mystery

The Pascal Mystery is a real historical event that actually happened — the passion, death, and resurrection of Jesus. It's an absolutely unique event. All other events in history happen once "and they pass away, swallowed up in the past" (CCC #1085). There's a key teaching of the Church on the Pascal Mystery that's absolutely awesome and critical for us to check out before we move on to the individual sacraments.

Check it out:

Catechism of the Catholic Church ➥ #1085

The event of Jesus' death and resurrection continues to have an effect on our lives.

Through the sacraments, we have access to this Pascal Mystery. That means we have the ability and the freedom to enter, to pass to and from the awesome power of the Pascal Mystery of Jesus. Yo, U got 2 believe!

Are U With Me?

You might be feelin that this is really awesome, or you might not be gettin it! This mystery stuff is a bit of a problem today in our modern rationalistic world. It's kind of like this: If we can't understand it, we don't go near it!

JP II points out that "modern rationalism does not tolerate mystery" — and boy, is he "right on the money"!

As Rabbi Abraham Heschel puts it, there is a specific meaning of mystery. "It is not a synonym for the unknown," he wrote in *God in Search of Man*, "but rather a name for a meaning which stands in relation to God."

Even people in the world of science get a sense of how important mystery is.

For example, you would think that the great discoveries made possible because of the Hubble Telescope would help us "settle the issue" of the mystery thing and outer space, right?

Nope! Sharon Begley pointed out in a *Newsweek* article (November 3, 1997, p. 37) that "paradoxically, the great measure of the Hubble's success may be that it is uncovering as many mysteries as it is solving." Kinda like the sacraments!

So now we're finally gettin ready to take a journey through the sacraments. First, we'll look at the sacraments of initiation: baptism confirmation, and Eucharist. Pope Paul VI said with these three sacraments we "receive in increasing measure the treasures of the divine life and advance toward the perfection of charity" (CCC #1212).

The Bath of Enlightenment

I love the "old school" language. I like the word "mysteries" better than "sacraments" — same thing! I like "bath of enlightenment" (CCC #1216) better than "baptism."

Jesus spoke about baptism when He commanded His disciples to baptize (see Matthew 28:19-20). Of course, He Himself was baptized (see Matthew 3:13-17), and He even baptized others (see John 3:22). So this is crucial!

What happens when we are baptized? What is different before and after?

The difference for us is supposed be somethin like this: "For once you were in darkness, but now in the Lord you are light. Live as children of light" (Ephesians 5:8).

Baptism not only cleanses us from sin but also incorporates us into the Church, makin us members of the Body of Christ (see CCC #1267). "So if anyone is in Christ, there is a new creation" (2 Corinthians 5:17).

How does this happen?

St. Paul says in Romans 6:3-4:

> Do you not know that all of us who have been baptized into Christ Jesus were baptized into his death? Therefore we have been buried with him by baptism into death, so that, just as Christ was raised from the dead by the glory of the Father, so we too might walk in newness of life.

St. Ambrose flat out says that baptism comes "from the cross of Christ, from his death. He dies for you. In him you are redeemed, in him you are saved."

I'm Going to Live Forever — in Christ!

The water symbolizes our burial into the death of Christ from which we rise up as a new creature. The anointing with the sacred chrism (the special oil used during baptism) represents our incorporation into Christ by the Holy Spirit.

I don't remember this happenin to me, but that's what was goin on.

Our connection with the supernatural life "has its roots in Baptism" (CCC #1266). Most of us have a hard enough time livin a natural life, and we're talkin about supernatural life? Water, oil — the basics. If we can live a more natural life, keepin it real and simple, and in some situations real simple, the supernatural life will take care of itself. U got 2 believe!

Jesus said, "The one who believes and is baptized will be saved; but the one who does not believe will be condemned" (Mark 16:16). That's why baptism is also called "the sacrament of faith" (CCC #1253). So this baptism thing is a big deal — in fact, it is a matter of life and death!

That's why the Church insists on instruction after baptism, "for the necessary flowering of baptismal grace in personal growth" (CCC #1231). It's necessary that we grow. We got to grow up, and we got to grow in our relationship with Jesus!

Is CCD class or your religion class gonna do it for you? It's suppose to help, but what else are you gonna do to grow? This growth thing is the work of a lifetime, so don't worry. Work at growin in your faith little by little, but grow!

Nobody can give you all the answers. It's more like our life has to become the answer as we follow Jesus every day! So let's get busy! That's why we renew our baptismal promises every year at the Easter Vigil. As the Church insists, "Faith must grow *after* Baptism" (CCC #1254). Your parents and godparents are suppose to help you grow in faith and in baptismal grace, but it doesn't always work out that way. So try not to waste time, but rather remain faithful to these demands of baptism.

Baptism seals us with an "indelible spiritual mark" of our belonging to Jesus. That means this spiritual mark can't be removed, washed away, or erased.

The Church teaches that "no sin can erase this mark, even if sin prevents Baptism from bearing the fruits of salvation" (CCC #1272).

We are sealed with the victory of Jesus over sin and death, yet at the same time we have to be really careful. While we proclaim the victory, there's a battle to be fought. Sin causes problems! But there ain't no sin or no problem we can't handle, with Jesus and the people He puts in our lives.

> *I love how the Church puts it, tellin us straight up, as you'll see when you check this out:*
>
> Catechism of the Catholic Church ➡ #1264
>
> *Some of the consequences of sin remain even after baptism.*

Becomin a Soldier of Christ

Now here's where the "old school" language kicks in — with the Sacrament of Confirmation. When I made my confirmation, I was told that I was becomin a "soldier of Christ Jesus."

Let's set the record straight: The only thing I was interested in when I made my confirmation was how much money I was gonna get so I could get a new skateboard! I wasn't interested in this soldier thing because I didn't know anything about the war!

But let me tell you — it's really different now! Now I know why the Church teaches that "Confirmation is necessary for the completion of baptismal grace" (CCC #1285).

When we get confirmed, we receive "the seal of the Holy Spirit." It's a sign of personal authority, which empowers us to share more fully in the mission of Jesus.

In ancient Rome, soldiers were marked with the seal of their leader — so we too are marked with the seal of our leader (check out CCC #1294-1295), Jesus Christ. "Like Baptism which it completes, Confirmation . . . imprints on the soul an *indelible spiritual mark*" (CCC #1304).

There Is a War Goin On — R U Ready for It?

In case you haven't noticed, there's a war goin on. I don't just mean the war between peoples and nations. I'm talkin about spiritual warfare, and we need to be strengthened and conditioned for the battle. I guess you could say that baptism equips us with the necessities for the battle, and that confirmation gets us ready to use the gifts received in combat.

What's the bottom line of this warfare? It is all about whether we want to be slaves or free, in the flesh or in Spirit, livin according to our sinful desires or livin as a member of the new creation.

St. Paul put it this way: "For freedom Christ has set us free. Stand firm, therefore, and do not submit again to a yoke of slavery" (Galatians 5:1).

The sinful nature wants one thing, and the Holy Spirit wants another thing for us. This conflict is the essence of the battle.

Check out again St. Paul's list of the acts of the sinful nature in Galatians 5:19-21. They're listed here in his order:

(1) Fornication *(sexual immorality)*, (2) Impurity *(includes dirty thoughts and jokes)*, (3) Licentiousness *(extreme indulgence in sensuality)*, (4) Idolatry, (5) Sorcery *(witchcraft)*, (6) Enmities *(hatred)*, (7) Strife *(especially from rivalries)*, (8) Jealousy, (9) Anger *(fits of rage)*, (10) Quarrels *(especially from selfish ambition)*, (11) Dissensions *(different negative opinions)*, (12) Factions *(cliques, self-seeking groups)*, (13) Envy, (14) Drunkenness, (15) Carousing *(orgies)*, (16) And things like these *(this covers all the bases in case you think he missed somethin!)*.

The other side of this struggle is the fruit of the Spirit in Galatians 5:22-23:

(1) Love, (2) Joy, (3) Peace, (4) Patience,
(5) Kindness, (6) Goodness, (7) Faithfulness,
(8) Gentleness, and (9) Self-control.

One basic fact about a war is that it involves conflict and hostility between opposing forces. Somebody wins and somebody loses.

In the case of the war I'm talkin about, Jesus has already won the victory over sin and death and all these opposing forces.

Confirmation helps us to share more completely in the victory of Jesus.

You might be sayin, "I'm too weak for this kinda thing."

And you're right — you are and so am I!

That's the point of confirmation. The Lord said, "Power is made perfect in weakness" (2 Corinthians 12:9). God gives us the power!

The Battle Is the Lord's!

Remember the story of David and Goliath?

There was a war between the Israelites and the Philistines.

Open the Bible and read this:

➡ 1 Samuel 17

The story of David and Goliath. Don't miss it!

Goliath was a champion, and the Bible tells us he was over nine feet tall. Yo, dude, that's big!

Little D (that's David) comes on the scene simply to bring food to the "big boys."

David was the Lord's anointed. So are we with confirmation. Let's call it the "Davidic sacrament." The anointing of the Holy Spirit makes us bold. If you haven't read the whole chapter from 1 Samuel 17, would you please stop and read it now?

Did you see what David was told? "You are not able to go against this Philistine to fight with him; for you are just a boy, and he has been a warrior from his youth" (1 Samuel 17:33). He was told he "couldn't do it"!

So many people (including ourselves when we talk to ourselves) tell us the same thing. Hey, we got to know we can't do it on our own. But yo, U got 2 believe! That's what confirmation can do for us if we're open and pray for the gifts of the Holy Spirit!

So what did Little D do? He said, "The LORD, who saved me from the paw of the lion and the paw of the bear, will save me from the hand of this Philistine" (1 Samuel 17:37).

David couldn't even wear the armor that Saul put on him because he was so small and weak! So he went just as he was, trustin in the Lord. With five smooth stones from the stream, his slingshot, and his trust in the Lord, off he went to do battle.

That's the key. We've got to go, just as we are, trustin in the Lord. It was the armor and strength of God that was David's real strength and protection. But was Little D ready or what? What about you? Are you ready? Are you ready to trust in the Lord and put on the armor of God?

David said to Goliath, "You come to me with sword and spear and javelin; but I come to you in the name of the LORD of hosts, the God of the armies of Israel, whom you have defied. This very day the LORD will deliver you into my hand, and I will strike you down . . . for the battle is the LORD's" (1 Samual 17:45-47). And with the first shot of his sling, David took care of business!

The Armor of God

David really took care of business because he trusted in the Lord and armored himself, first of all, with the armor of God. We have the fullness of that in Jesus Christ, who comes to us from the family line of David. Confirmation is all about equippin us with the full armor of God.

The battle is the Lord's, and when we put on the full armor of God we're ready to deal with all kinds of stuff that on our own we can't even begin to think about dealin with. Obviously, we're not fightin a physical battle: "For our struggle is not against enemies of blood and flesh, but against the rulers, against the authorities, against the cosmic powers of this present darkness, against the spiritual forces of evil in the heavenly places" (Ephesians 6:12). But yo, U got 2 believe!

Check this out:

⇒ Ephesians 6:13-18

Paul describes the armor of God that we are to put on daily.

Be sure you pray with this, think about it, pray for it, and talk it up with your friends and youth group. (And if you don't have a youth group, talk to some folks and start one. You can do it!)

The Most Blessed Sacrament

While confirmation is necessary for the completion of the graces we get at baptism, it's the Most Blessed Sacrament, the Eucharist, that "completes Christian initiation" (CCC #1322).

The Eucharist is called "the Most Blessed Sacrament" because "it is the Sacrament of sacraments" (CCC #1330). It's the greatest sacrament because the Greatest Love is really and truly present. That's the Lord Jesus.

There is no greater love than the Love that Jesus loved us with. No matter what else is said here, our bein saved by Jesus is all about us bein loved so much by Him.

Remember, Jesus is God, God is love, and Jesus is really and truly present — Body, Blood, Soul, and Divinity — in the Most Blessed Sacrament. Case closed!

Are our hearts open to this gift? That's another story! It's really "*the* story"! Opening our hearts to so great a love!

We're not talkin about a symbol here, but the real-deal presence of Jesus. I put it this way in my song "Take My Heart," from my CD of the same name:

Sometimes ya wonder about the mystery of the Bread.
The real deal Presence, no trip for the head.
Ya wanna live forever, ya gotta be fed.
His Body and Blood, (SORRY!) it's what the Master said.

Feel His Love, feel the Power, as ya worship and adore.
Ya wanna live a new life and sin no more?
Let Him play His part, don't let Him wait to start.
Ya gotta pray — take my heart.

Sometimes we would rather just hold on. What a pity.
I know it seems easier to hold on than to let go. Anyway,
let's get back to work.

Key Teachings About the Eucharist

Let me hit ya with a bunch of key teachings of the Church about the Holy Eucharist:

- "The Eucharist is 'the source and summit of the Christian life' " (CCC #1324).
- The Eucharist is the cause of communion that we have with God and each other. It is what makes us the People of God (check out CCC #1325).
- When we celebrate the Mass, our celebration is one with the heavenly liturgy and anticipates the eternal life we hope to share with God and His saints (check out CCC #1326).
- The Eucharist makes present the sacrifice of Christ's death on the cross and adds to it our own sacrifices as an offering (check out CCC #1330).
- Jesus presides invisibly over every eucharistic celebration; the human minister — whether bishop or priest — represents Him (check out CCC #1348).
- The purpose of every Mass is communion of the faithful with Christ, and in receiving communion the faithful receive Christ himself (check out CCC #1382).
- Every Mass is celebrated in communion with the entire Body of Christ, both living and dead, both in heaven and on earth (check out CCC #1354).

This is awesome stuff! So tell me, why is church or goin to Mass borin? Believe me, it's because of us! There ain't nothin borin about Him! We're not aware of what's really goin on.

Don't get me wrong. We sometimes get a lot of the wrong kind of help from priests and congregations that lack a real passion for Jesus. That lack of passion expresses itself in bad preachin, bad singin, lack of energy in the readin of the Word of God in church, bad fellowship before and durin and after Mass, and even in inexcusably bad sound systems! The list can go on.

That's not the point! The point is, "in the Eucharist the Church is as it were at the foot of the cross with Mary, united with the offering and intercession of Christ" (CCC #1370). Chew on that for a while, and say good-bye to the "Mass is boring" thing! Time to wake up, folks! U got 2 believe!

The Holy Sacrifice of the Mass

The Eucharist involves many dimensions of human life: celebration, gathering, and meal, just to mention a few. The biggie is that the Eucharist is a sacrifice. That's why we say "the Holy Sacrifice of the Mass."

The reason for this is that, whenever Mass is celebrated, the onetime sacrifice of Jesus on the cross is made present at that Mass in an unbloody manner.

Check this out:

Catechism of the Catholic Church ➡ #1366

Jesus wished to leave us a visible sacrifice for our sins.

You got to keep readin and re-readin what the Church is sayin here to really get this. We keep forgettin! We're talkin here bout the greatest gift and mystery this side of heaven.

So what did you expect? Plug and play? Our minds are conditioned by this "plug and play," got-to-get-it right-away thing: immediate gratification. Not so with the Holy Eucharist, and not so with anything else in this life that's really worth your while.

My Body Given Up for You

On Holy Thursday, Jesus instituted the Eucharist. He said, "Take this, all of you, and eat it: this is my body which will be given up for you." Then He took the cup and said, " Take this, all of you, and drink from it: this is the cup of my blood, the blood of the new and everlasting covenant. It will be shed for you and for all so that sins may be forgiven. Do this in memory of me."

The day after He said this, He did it — gave up His body and shed His blood that we might be saved by so great a love.

Just remember. When you forget, remember. The great mystery of the Eucharist is so much bigger that you, me, your parish, and our limited experience of reality.

Check this out: The Church teaches that in the Holy Sacrifice of the Mass, all of "creation loved by God is presented to the Father" (CCC #1359) through the Paschal Mystery (the death and resurrection of Christ). I could go on forever about the Eucharist. Hopefully, I will — and so will you! Know what I'm sayin? Jesus said, "Whoever eats of this bread will live forever" (John 6:51).

I want to share with you what JP said when I was in Rome on October 11, 2000, for his general audience. Stick with this and everything will be alright:

United to the sacrifice of Christ, the Church in the Eucharist gives voice to the praise of the entire creation. This must be corresponded to by the determination of each of the faithful to offer his existence, his "body" as St. Paul says, in a living communion with Christ. In this way, one unique life unites God and man, Christ crucified and risen for all, and the disciple called to give himself totally to him.

If we ain't gettin a sense of the real presence of Jesus inside the church, we ain't gonna get a sense of the real presence of Jesus outside the church. This is the "living communion with Christ" that the Holy Father is talkin about, which creates a bond of solidarity with all people — to be aware of the presence of Jesus in the poor and suffering, and in all peoples. Remember, rich people suffer too.

So if you're bored with Jesus inside the church, you're probably missin Him outside the church. Only you can make the difference. Will you?

Havin taken a look at the sacraments of initiation — baptism, confirmation, and the Eucharist — we now will look at the sacraments of healing: penance and the anointing of the sick. But before we move on, I should say that even though the Eucharist isn't classified as a sacrament of healing, it has awesome healing power. Check out what St. Thomas Aquinas has to say about it: "No other sacrament has greater healing power; through it sins are purged away, virtues are increased, and the soul is enriched with an abundance of every spiritual gift."

Penance and Reconciliation

The Sacrament of Penance and Reconciliation has a bunch of different names: the sacrament of conversion, confession, forgiveness, and even the sacrament of healing (see CCC #1423 and #1424).

What we call it ain't the important thing. What is important is that we practice it.

Check it out — it's free! Don't cost you any money to get forgiven and to receive healin.

How often should you go? Once a month is a good minimum. Everybody pays the phone bill and their rent once a month. Well, almost everybody. At least they're expected to. So why don't we take care of our soul at least once a month with this awesome sacrament?

I go to confession about every two weeks. It's absolutely awesome! Goin to confession on a regular basis is really important. Even if you don't have any big sins (mortal sins).

The Church teaches that "the regular confession of our venial sins helps us form our conscience, fight against evil tendencies, let ourselves be healed by Christ and progress in the life of the Spirit" (CCC #1458). So there ya go!

One reason why some people don't go to confession might be because many priests don't go to confession themselves. And if they're not goin to confession, they not gonna encourage you to go to confession. Some priests might just be a little bit lazy. It happens. If you go to confession, then they got to work, right?

But for most priests, it's a great joy to be involved in this sacrament — from both sides of the confessional screen! I'm talkin from experience here.

Check out what the Church teaches: "Priests must encourage the faithful to come to the sacrament of Penance and must make themselves available to celebrate this sacrament each time Christians reasonably ask for it" (CCC #1464). So if confession isn't available at your parish, go to the priest and ask for it! You have every right to do so!

What Do I Confess?

It's all about conversion. Remember what JP said about conversion: It's a lifelong process.

Even with all the amazing graces of baptism, confirmation, and the Eucharist, the Church teaches us that the frailty and weakness of our human nature remains such that with the grace of Jesus in this sacrament we "may prove [ourselves] in the struggle of Christian life" (CCC #1426).

Lots of people don't wanna hear about sin or deal with it, but you got to let go of your sins in order to move on! Amen!

So what do I confess? Big sins only? Only those big, nasty, don't-wanna-mention–em sins? Do I have to mention the small stuff, over and over again, and again and again?

Yes.

St. Augustine puts it well in his homily on the First Letter of St. John:

> A man, so long as he bears the flesh, cannot but have some, at any rate, light sins. But these that we call light, you should not make light of. If you make light of them when you weigh them, be afraid when you count them. Many light sins make one huge sin: many drops fill a river; a great number of grains make a pile. And what hope is there? Before all, confession. . . .

God's Power Given to Men

Lots of folks have a problem with this sacrament: "I ain't tellin my sins to no priest. He can't forgive my sins."

Guess what? That's right! He can't.

The Church teaches that God alone can forgive sins! (Check out CCC #1441.)

But check this out. In Mark 2:10, Jesus said that "the Son of Man has authority on earth to forgive sins." And by virtue of His divine authority, Jesus has given this power to priests to exercise in His name! (Did you check out CCC #1441 yet?)

Remember, sacraments are powers that come forth from Christ, and they are actions of the Holy Spirit.

Here are a few key Scripture passages to keep in mind when it comes to the Sacrament of Penance:

"I will give you the keys of the kingdom of heaven, and whatever you bind on earth will be bound in heaven, and whatever you loose on earth will be loosed in heaven." — *Matthew 16:19*

In this passage, Jesus gives Peter the power to loose and bind with divine power.

> "Truly I tell you, whatever you bind on earth will be bound in heaven, and whatever you loose on earth will be loosed in heaven." — *Matthew 18:18*
>
> *Here the same power is given to the Church.*
>
> "Receive the Holy Spirit. If you forgive the sins of any, they are forgiven them; if you retain the sins of any, they are retained." — *John 20:22-23*
>
> *The apostles are given the power to forgive sins by the risen Lord.*

Only Jesus has the authority to forgive sins, and only Jesus had the authority to give this authority to His priests.

I can understand how someone can feel uncomfortable confessin their sins. But this is somethin you got to do! I wasn't born feelin good about confessin my sins — I grew into it through practice.

Listen to St. Jerome: "If a sick man is ashamed to show his wound to the doctor, the medicine cannot heal what it does not know."

I like to put it this way: Roaches come out only in the nighttime! In other words, we need to expose our sins to the light of Christ, and that means bringin them to confession where you can say them.

When it comes to sin, you got to name it, claim it, and tame it in Jesus! If you wanna bust the boogeyman, turn the lights on! Once you get used to it, it's absolutely awesome!

Even when you go to confession and receive absolution (the prayer of cleansin), the disorder that sin has caused still remains. The Church teaches that "absolution takes away sin, but it does not remedy all the disorders sin has caused" (CCC #1459). So we need to do penance and be open to the special grace of this sacrament for the healing of the bad effects of sin. It takes lots of time, but it works!

Just in case you don't know, every priest is bound by the sacramental seal of confession. That means that the priest is "bound under very severe penalties to keep absolute secrecy regarding the sins that his penitents have confessed to him" *(CCC #1467). There are "no exceptions."*

If a priest has ever been rude, nasty, or kind of stupid to you in confession, I want to apologize as a brother priest on his behalf. Don't let him or anybody else keep you from comin to Jesus in this awesome sacrament. In fact, the Church teaches that the minister of this sacrament — the priest — "should unite himself to the intention and charity of Christ" (CCC #1466). That means that at least he should be a decent human being! Actually, he should be very compassionate, extremely lovin and understandin, full of mercy, challengin, and, hopefully, with a bit of good advice. All of this is for "an increase of spiritual strength for the Christian battle" (CCC #1496).

Remember that the level of your preparation is gonna determine the level of your celebration. You got to prepare yourself. From the time I walk out of the confessional until the next time I walk in, I'm preparin for the sacrament. Then when I go to confession I really zero in on where my heart is hurtin, where I messed up, and I bring it all to Jesus. It takes me about five minutes. I do most of the talkin, then the priest offers me a little word of encouragement, advice, penance, and then I'm off, back to the battlefield!

Examining Your Conscience

Remember the examination of conscience? That's what I'm talkin bout!

The Church teaches that when we approach this sacrament we should first prepare ourselves by examinin our conscience in the light of the Scriptures. In other words, when I hear how Jesus describes His followers, how do I measure up?

Here are some Scripture chapters for you to use to help you examine your conscience.

Matthew 5-7
Romans 12-15
1 Corinthians 12-13
Galatians 5
Ephesians 4-6

Reflect on the Scriptures and ask yourself how your relationship with the Lord is goin. (There's a detailed examination of conscience in the Appendix.) When you finish, go take the plunge into the awesome mercy, forgiveness, healin, and amazin grace of this awesome sacrament.

Anointing of the Sick

Lots of times we don't really appreciate what we have until we lose it, especially our health. This is somethin you don't think about too much when you're young and healthy, or even old and healthy!

When was the last time you thanked God that you could breath freely, or chew, or walk without pain? Did you ever have a kidney infection? I did. When was the last time you thanked God that you could go to the bathroom without feelin you were gonna die? Don't laugh! If you ever get a kidney infection, you'll be cryin! Just be grateful and thank Him! Oh yeah! Thank you, Lord!

I think one of the reasons why we don't suffer well and find meaning in our sufferin is because we are ungrateful for who we are and what we have. That lack of gratitude keeps us from unitin our sufferin with the sufferin of Jesus. We can become so insensitive to the pain and illness of others.

By His passion, death, and resurrection, Jesus gives us new meaning to sufferin. Jesus had a special love for those who were sick. He identifies with them totally: "I was sick and you took care of me" (Matthew 25:36). Because of Jesus, Christians have tried to comfort the sick through the centuries.

Through the Sacrament of the Anointing of the Sick, the sick person "receives the strength and the gift of uniting himself more closely to Christ's Passion." That's how sufferin acquires new meanin, by being united with Jesus in His sufferin. Our sufferin then becomes "a participation in the saving work of Jesus" (CCC #1521).

If you ever have to go into surgery for anything or you find yourself real sick, don't hesitate to call the priest (or have someone else call him if you're too sick to do it) to receive this great sacrament of healing! But don't wait to get sick to get close to Jesus!

Sacraments of Service and Communion

Now, speakin bout getting closer, the last two sacraments — holy orders and matrimony — are all about gettin close and stayin close. They're referred to as sacraments ordered to the service of communion.

I guess you could even say that all the sacraments are about gettin us close, and keepin us close, to Jesus and one another. After all, the word *communion* means to be in union with and to have intimate fellowship or communication. Break up the word: *com* (with), *union* (two becoming one).

You might be sayin, "Yeah, I can see that with marriage for sure, but not with the priesthood."

Well, hold on a minute! Jesus was all about communion, all about bein one with the Father, and you and me and everybody and the priesthood are all about Jesus! So there you have it!

In John 10:30, Jesus said, "The Father and I are one." Jesus even takes it further! Check this out: "Whoever believes in me believes not in me but in him who sent me. And whoever sees me sees him who sent me" (John 12:44-45). Yo, U really got 2 believe!

If you could believe it, and I can, Jesus takes it even further! It's not just about Him and the Father; He includes us in that awesome and mysterious communion: "Very truly, I tell you, whoever receives one whom I send receives me; and whoever receives me receives him who sent me" (John 13:20).

So it ain't just Jesus and the Father, but anyone that Jesus sends. This includes His priests — the ministry of Jesus and His Church! You learn the most about a person when you watch them pray. Take your Bible out and look at Jesus as He prays.

Read this:

➡ John 17

The prayer of Jesus.

So there you go. Read and re-read — pray, pray, and pray with Jesus in John 17. The whole chapter! He prayed that the world may believe. That's why I'm tellin you again and again: U got 2 believe! Jesus prayed for this, and also that we may be brought to "complete unity."

Oh, my Jesus, come and squeeze us! How badly do we need that love. We got to believe that the Father loves us even as He loved Jesus. That's what Jesus is prayin for. That's the essence, the bottom line of this communion. It's got to manifest itself in our livin in the world. I need to do a whole book on the service of communion — our service to God, to one another, to the Church, to the poor, and to everyone. Maybe that's the next book. Whatever!

Holy Orders

The Sacrament of Holy Orders is the means Jesus chose to continue the mission given to the apostles until the end of time (check out CCC #1536).

Pope, cardinal, bishop, and deacon all flow from this sacrament. It's all about Jesus! "The sacrament of Holy Orders communicates a 'sacred power' which is none other than that of Christ" (CCC #1551).

Holy orders serves communion through the priesthood, as the priest acts in the Person of Christ and proclaims His Paschal Mystery. A little Latin here: *in Persona Christi* ("in the Person of Christ"). As a priest, I see it this way: In my manhood, priesthood, and neighborhood, it's Jesus! Jesus! Jesus!

Check this out:

Catechism of the Catholic Church   ➥ #1566

Priests draw their strength from the one sacrifice of Jesus.

Maybe God is callin you to serve Him as a priest in His Church. Don't be afraid. Remember Little D? It's not about you or me; it's about the power of Christ!

If you are unsure — or are sure — check out a vocation director (someone who can help you discern whether God is callin you) for a religious order that interests you, or for servin in your own diocese where you live. Don't be afraid!

Sacrament of Matrimony

The Sacrament of Matrimony is all about servin in communion too. It's "a partnership of the whole of life" (CCC #1601).

Usually with this sacrament folks think, "Now I can have all the sex I want and nobody can say nothin!"

While in a certain sense that may be true, listen to the wisdom of one of my professors in the seminary. In speakin about married couples, he said, "If you never have to say no (no to havin sex), your yes won't mean very much."

Sex outside of marriage is a sin. Sex within marriage is for the good of the spouses — the husband and wife — as well as for the pro-creation of children. What a gift!

The two shall become one flesh. Jesus reminds us that this teachin goes way back to the beginnin:

"But from the beginning of creation, 'God 'made them male and female.' 'For this reason a man shall leave his father and mother and be joined to his wife, and the two shall become one flesh.' So they are no longer two, but one flesh. Therefore what God has joined together, let no one separate." (Mark 10: 6-9)

In Ephesians 5:22-31, St. Paul shows how marriage serves communion by comparin it to the relationship of love between Jesus and His Church. In verse 32, he concludes, "This is a great mystery." In other words, it's a great sacrament. This is a profound mystery because of Jesus, who, along with the husband and wife, is the third and invisible partner.

Read this:

Catechism of the Catholic Church ➡ #1642

The Church teaches that Christ gives a couple strength.

Difficult Situations

But as you know, it doesn't always work out that way. Yes, marriage is a great mystery, the two becomin one flesh. Unfortunately, they don't always stay that way, even though God joined them together.

The Church teaches that there are some situations where living together becomes practically impossible, and here "the Church permits the physical *separation* of the couple" (CCC #1649). Worse still, sometimes there's divorce. This causes even bigger problems, as way too many of you know by experience. But Jesus can help you through all that. U got 2 believe!

Check it out! Marriage is suppose to help men and women to overcome all that threatens their union — stuff like discord, attitudes of domination and control, infidelity, jealousy, conflicts, and a thousand other dangers! This union is supposed to be forever — "until death do us part" — as the marriage vows say. But when you're not used to turnin to Jesus when strugglin to overcome difficulties and challenges early on in life, you're not gonna know how to lean on Him later on in life. Believe it!

That's why the Church teaches us, "To heal the wounds of sin, man and woman need the help of the grace that God in his infinite mercy never refuses them" (CCC #1608). The problem, as usual, is with us, not with God. Try not to waste your time. It's all good. God is good. He will help you to move on when necessary and to stay close to Him through it all. U got 2 believe!

Seekin God's Help in Marriage

Here's a great line from the teaching of the Church: "It can seem difficult, even impossible, to bind oneself for life to another human being" (CCC #1648). No kiddin! That's why Jesus needs to be welcomed as, and remain as, the third invisible partner in the Sacrament of Matrimony. With Him, all things are possible — even having a blessed and happy marriage.

I've seen a lot of messed-up situations. I've seen people — especially the kids, who suffer the most — move on and beyond some serious problems. I've also seen a lot of great situations, which are so awesome to see. God is workin in all of that!

Marriage is suppose to help men and women overcome "self-absorption, egoism, pursuit of one's own pleasure, and to open oneself to the other, to mutual aid and to self-giving" (CCC 1609).

It is by followin Christ, renouncin themselves, and takin up their crosses that spouses will be able to receive the original meanin of marriage and live it with the help of Christ. "This grace of Christian marriage is a fruit of Christ's cross, the source of all Christian life" (CCC #1615).

Like I said, it ain't necessarily so! If men and women are not alive in Christ before they're married, or don't become alive in Christ when they're married, they are gonna have a hard time makin it.

As with all the other sacraments, preparation plays a key role. Y'all are supposed to be gettin help from your pastors, and from the Christian community as the family of God.

Lots of you are probably sayin, "What's that?" Hopefully, we can change that by acceptin Christ and bein there for one another. Commitment. Let's face it: You might not be seein that kind of help around too much. And when it's there, most folks don't know how to accept it anyhow!

There's a very easy, but wrong, attitude: "I can do it on my own!" No, you can't! No I can't! It's more like "We can do it" — through, with, and in Christ.

The Christian values of marriage and family need to be held up high so our young people can be taught. Taught by example. It's difficult to find that kind of teachin out there today — by example. But keep lookin, cause it's out there for sure! And if you don't find it, ask the Lord to help you be that example for others. He will see you through.

The Lord and His Church are workin "much more so in our era when many young people experience broken homes which no longer sufficiently assure this initiation" (CCC #1632). The Bible tells us in Romans 5:20 that "where sin increased, grace abounded all the more."

Lots of problems? More grace! Jesus, we put our trust in U!

Conclusion

Remember, Jesus gave each of the sacraments to us as a way to enrich our life and keep us close to Him. Prepare yourself for an awesome encounter with Jesus, and you will not be disappointed! It's all one in Christ! Count on it!

Therefore, since we are surrounded by so great a cloud of witnesses, let us also lay aside every weight and the sin that clings so closely, and let us run with perseverance the race that is set before us, looking to Jesus the pioneer and perfecter of our faith, who for the sake of the joy that was set before him endured the cross, disregarding its shame, and has taken his seat at the right hand of the throne of God.

Hebrews 12:1-2

CHAPTER 5

Community: F.A.M.I.L.Y.

How Do U Spell Community?

How do you spell *community*? F.A.M.I.L.Y.
The letters stand for:

F   Forget
A   About
M   Me
I   I
L   Love
Y   You

Forget about me, I love you — Family. That's community!

The Catholic Twist

No, it ain't a new dance! The Catholic twist on this community thing goes somethin like this: With things that are essential, we must have unity; with the non-essentials, we can have diversity. This was somethin that St. Augustine said a long, long time ago!

The most basic example is the Eucharist.

If you travel, you may notice that Mass might be said in different languages and with different music. Some churches might have lots of flowers; some none. You may also notice lots of styles based on culture.

Yet no matter where the Eucharist is celebrated, there is real bread and real wine that becomes the real Body, Blood, Soul, and Divinity of Jesus Christ! And that's what really matters — Jesus!

So the essential thing is not a "thing" at all but a Person — Jesus. He brings us together and holds us together. Here goes Jesus: "The kingdom of heaven is like a net that was thrown into the sea and caught fish of every kind" (Matthew 13:47). All kinds of stuff in community! Know what I'm sayin?

The key in this passage of Scripture for me is that the Kingdom is made up of "all kinds of fish." That means what it says: *all* kinds! Some ya like, and some ya don't. Some like you, and others don't. Are you feelin me? Oh yeah, baby!

Only Jesus can help us to overcome ourselves and all adversity and conflict — and there is plenty of that! It takes all kinds, and God gives everybody a chance — even many chances . . . like 70 x 7, which basically means don't calculate but contemplate how awesome God is! Sometimes it gets really complicated!

Guess what? We got to be like God and give in and forgive, and that takes some forgettin about ourselves and lovin our brothers and sisters! I'm talkin bout bein Family!

It Ain't Easy!

For us, it's all about trainin, trainin, and more trainin; to mold, form, and re-form our way of thinking to God's way of thinkin — the work of a lifetime! Stinkin thinkin leads to stinkin feelin, which leads to stinkin behavior — so be careful! To live in community requires a change in the way we think, especially when all we're thinkin about is ourselves! Time to grow up, folks — that's for all of us! Don't worry! Pray every day and take it one step at a time.

Be Like Mike — Be Disciplined

Michael Jordan was already a very famous and great basketball player for many years, but he couldn't consistently hit the three-point shot. So what did he do? Stay away from the three-point line? No way, José! No such thought!

Rather, MJ committed himself with lots of discipline. In the off-season and durin the season, he practiced, practiced, and practiced, probably hundreds of shots a day, to perfect the three-point shot. Awesome!

The greatest player worked hard and became even greater! He wasn't just thinkin about his own achievement, but he was plannin for his team to win even more championships! Forgettin about himself, he was thinkin about his team stayin focused on the goal.

I'm sure that at first Michael didn't have a pleasant experience with all of that discipline. But I bet ya he loved it when those shots started droppin and he took home more championship rings!

Discipline — the Key to Livin in Community

That's why the Bible says that "discipline always seems painful rather than pleasant at the time, but later it yields the peaceful fruit of righteousness to those who have been trained by it" (Hebrews 12:11).

You can certainly call MJ's game "righteous"! Yes, great God-given talent and, yes, an awesome, committed, dedicated, and disciplined work ethic! That's the winnin combo! Are you gettin it yet? It's never too late.

Time to consult with Brother Webster, who says that discipline *is*
- Trainin that corrects, molds, or perfects the mental faculties or moral character.
- Self-control.

Discipline *can also mean*
- To punish.

In Hebrew's 12:7, we are told to "endure trials for the sake of discipline." Can't really talk about community without talkin about trials.

Community can be a safe place where we can be who we really are, a place where we can be loved and accepted. This is true. But it ain't gonna work unless those in the community make a gift of themselves. Along with bein loved and accepted, we have to be acceptin and lovin.

Imagine if everybody just wanted to be loved and accepted, and everybody wasn't tryin to be acceptin and lovin? Disaster!

People in community always need to change. But, unfortunately, most of us change rarely and slowly. That's just how it is. It's got to start with us! One step at a time.

Cardinal Newman said somethin really great: "In a higher world it is otherwise, but here below to live is to change, and to be perfect is to change often." So don't bug out if you or somebody else has to keep on changin and makin adjustments. It's part of the deal.

Forget About ME!

Let's take a look at the "forgettin about me" part of F.A.M.I.L.Y.

First of all, it presumes that you have a self that knows you are loved by God and others. In other words, before you forget about yourself, you got to have love and respect for yourself.

Wait a minute! You might be sayin, "Ain't that selfish?"

It can be, but it doesn't have to be. Let's call it a "Gospel-enlightened self-love."

Jesus said that the greatest commandment is to " 'love the Lord your God with all your heart, and with all your soul, and with all your mind.' . . . And a second is like it: 'You shall love your neighbor as yourself' " (Matthew 22:37, 39).

As with any project you may be plannin, you have to keep the goal in mind and work backwards. So that means this: With the greatest commandment, the goal is to love God with all our heart, soul, and mind — and our neighbor as ourself.

So we begin this lifelong project of lovin God and others by first lovin ourselves.

1 John 4:19 tells us, "We love because he first loved us." It's all about God!

And check this out: If you say, "Well, Fadda, God couldn't love me because of this or that," you need to go back to the first chapter and start readin all over again! God's love for us is greater than anything we can possibly ever do or think that would prevent it from penetratin our hearts. Remember, Jesus died to save us from all of our "this or thats"!

Lovin God Means Lovin Others Too!

Sometimes I meet people who say they love God but can't stand some of their family members, or some of the kids in their class, or some of the people in their neighborhood.

Whoa! We can't cop out and say, "It's alright cause I love God." Hold on, Charlie!

Check it out:

Those who say, "I love God," and hate their brothers or sisters, are liars; for those who do not love a brother or sister whom they have seen, cannot love God whom they have not seen. The commandment we have from him is this: those who love God must love their brothers and sisters also.

— *1 John 4:20-21*

St. Augustine puts it like this: "Love of God is the first to be commanded, but the love of neighbor is the first to be put into practice."

How Do You Live It?

OK, so I have to love my neighbor!
The bigger question here is: How do I do it?

My way of spellin *community*, and understanding it and livin it (F.A.M.I.L.Y.), is based on the song "F.A.M.I.L.Y. (In-Laws)," from my *Sacro Song* CD. Let me drop Verse 1 for you:

Forget about me because I love you.
I wanna put ya in my family and love ya through.
A family community ya give ya love free,
That's the kind of family we gotta work to be.
With the love from above that's how a family is found.
Through the problems and the pain there's enough love to
     go around.
Pray for all the people give ya self in all ya do.
Forget about me because I love you.

Dr. Martin Luther King, Jr., had a great insight that can be extremely useful to help us build community and to live as F.A.M.I.L.Y. He said, "Life's most persistent and urgent question is: What are you doing for others?" The next time you're feelin sorry for yourself, ask yourself this question. It's a good reality check. Before we go on to some other dimensions of community, we got to pile up some stuff about the bottom line.

The bottom line of it all is *love*. A very misused and abused word. Check out most of the songs you hear and movies you watch. (You're probably not readin too many books. Not a good idea. There are a lot of great books — read only the best stuff!). We're talkin bout love, the love that's the core of the Gospel and all the stuff that goes with it.

If we could get with this and stick with it, we'd have awesome improvements in our communities, in our homes, in the Church, in the schools and workplaces, and in the street. Fa real! We would really be makin lots of progress livin out the vision and joy of F.A.M.I.L.Y.

Jesus' Model of Community

Jesus gave His life that we might be one. In His teachin, He also instructed us with a way to really build community, to live out F.A.M.I.L.Y.

Check out these principles and look up the Scriptures that back them up!

The Lord's Rule of Community Life

1. Don't judge others! (Check out Matthew 7:1-5.)
2. Practice the Golden Rule: Treat others in the way you would want to be treated. (Check out Matthew 7:12.)
3. Love your enemies, forgive everyone who wrongs you! (Check out Luke 6:27-38.)

That's a whole lot right there!

We're all so broken. It all can seem so hard, and it is hard — but with God, all things are possible!

We have to remember it's not about us, but about our trust in God. He can provide the strength we need to make a difference, to help ourselves and others along the way. That's the key! To learn how to rely on God. To put our trust in God.

It takes time. Community takes time, and most of the time as with most things we want everything right away. Fast food and instant community. You can get yourself some fast food. Not so with community! No instant community. No instant holiness.

TIME OUT! According to Dr. Scott Peck, in his book The Different Drum: Community Making *and Peace:*

It takes a great deal of work for a group of strangers to achieve the safety of community. Once they succeed, however, it is as if the floodgates were opened. As soon as it's safe to speak one's heart, as soon as most people in the group know they will be listened to and accepted for themselves, years and years of pent up frustration and hurt and guilt and grief come pouring out . . . the walls come tumbling down. And as they tumble, as the love and acceptance escalates, as the mutual intimacy multiplies, true healing and converting begins. Old wounds are healed, old resentments forgiven, old resistances overcome. Fear is replaced by hope.

This all sounds good, really challengin, and a bit overwhelmin! Amen? So what do we do? Forget about community? Let's start with a different question. Actually, let's ask the basic question given to us by JP at World Youth Day 2000 in Rome.

JP II Has a Question 4 U!

At World Youth Day 2000, John Paul II was talkin about the times we live in and how they call us to make "decisive choices," choices about the direction of our studies, work, and our role in society as well our role in the Church.

The Pope boiled it down to this:

> It is important to realize that among the many questions surfacing in your minds, the decisive ones are not about "what." The basic question is "who" — "who" am I to go to, "who" am I to follow, "to whom" should I entrust my life?

It's Jesus.

What the Pope is sayin is that it's all about Jesus. This is what I've been tryin to say all along. This is the key question for community — not so much "What do we have to do?" but rather "Who will we follow, who will guide us in the way we live our lives?" Will we really try to trust Jesus and give our lives to Him? Again and again and again?

Once we make this decision for Jesus, we can truly begin to build community. This decision ain't no one-shot deal; it's a daily choice. We have to choose Christ and live out that choice by how we treat those we meet every day.

As we choose Christ and live from this decision every day, we gradually become free from the need to be at the center of everything, free from the fear of makin a gift of ourselves. This happens only as we come to know ourselves as loved by Jesus. He loves us with an everlastin love. He loves us all the way! His love can make us capable of lovin even without limits! This is where the real fun begins!

TIME OUT! Check this out, from the Vatican Congregation for Institutes of Consecrated Life and Societies of Apostolic Life:

Christ gives a person two basic certainties: the certainty of being infinitely loved and the certainty of being capable of loving without limits. Nothing except the Cross of Christ can give in a full and definitive way these two certainties and the freedom they bring. . . . [Those who allow themselves to be guided by Christ] learn rather to love as Christ loved them, with that love which now is poured forth in their hearts, making them capable of forgetting themselves and giving themselves as the Lord did.

— Fraternal Life in Community #22

To love without limits! Can you feel the necessity for the divine life? O Lord, have mercy! Alleluia!

Forgive — Forget — Let Go!

I guess if you had to name the most difficult area of community livin, it would probably be forgiveness. It's without a doubt the most important too.

Jesus taught us how to pray as individuals with a community focus. He taught us to pray "Our Father . . ." — remindin us that we are one family. Notice somethin else about the prayer. He hit the nail right on the head with the petition "forgive us our trespasses as we forgive those who trespass against us." Boom!

We're askin God to forgive us as much as, or as little as, we forgive others! In other words, "Forget about me because I love you" becomes the key to my forgivin you, which becomes the degree for how much I'm gonna be forgiven!

Whoa! Are you startin to see how this whole thing works? Jesus said, "The measure you give will be the measure you get" (Matthew 7:2). There ya go! R U feelin me?

As we begin and continue to grow on the journey of buildin community, we will find forgiveness at the heart of it.

TIME OUT! Jean Vanier has lots of experience with buildin community. Let's give him a listen and hope we can learn from his experience, as told in his book From Brokenness to Community:

At the heart of community, as we learn to care for our brothers and sisters, there is forgiveness. Reconciliation is at the heart of community. To grow in love means that we become men and women of forgiveness, of reconciliation. The heart of the message of Christ, its fundamental newness, is the promise of an inner strength which comes with the gift of the Spirit, the Holy Spirit, the third person of the family of God loving inside of us, so that we can forgive and be forgiven. When I say that forgiveness is at the heart of community, I do not mean we have to learn to say simply, "You're a nuisance but I forgive you." It means discovering that I too am in part the cause of your being a nuisance, because I have dominated you, hurt you, brought fear up in you or because I haven't listened to you, or was not open to you. Forgiveness is not just saying, "I forgive you because you slammed the door." It's also: "I'm working on changing myself, because I have hurt you." We're all wounded people, and so consciously or unconsciously we can and do hurt each other. At the heart of a caring community is forgiveness, one to another. This is a principle of growth. We forgive each other because we yearn to grow and to become like Jesus.

The followin lines from the *Catechism* are some of my most favorites. In commentin on the petition for forgiveness in the prayer Jesus taught us, the Church teaches, "*It is not in our power* not to feel or to forget an offence; but the heart that offers itself to the Holy Spirit turns injury into compassion and purifies the memory in transforming the hurt into intercession" (CCC #2843).

It Is Not in Our Power

I think these are my favorite six words in the whole *Catechism of the Catholic Church*: "It is not in our power!" This means that we are powerless.

Powerless, but not hopeless! Powerless over what?

Powerless over our inability to forgive and forget. This is where the divine life has to kick in! The Holy Spirit, the Lord and Giver of Life, comes to our aid with divine help. All we have to do is ask and believe. U got 2 believe!

The Holy Spirit turns injury into compassion, our ability to suffer with others, to see and feel things from their side of the fence, to walk in somebody else's shoes. The Holy Spirit also turns the hurt into intercession. We no longer have to waste the pain, but can pray for the people involved in the difficulty. We can find meaning in our sufferin. This is good news!

As the Bible says in Romans 8:28, "We know that all things work together for good for those who love God, who are called according to his purpose." That purpose is for us to be at peace with ourselves and with one another. So let's not waste all the pain we sometimes feel; we can minimize the pain we cause to others. With God's help, and lots of discipline on our part, let's try to make a gift of our heart, as it is, to the Holy Spirit and give Him permission to make love happen "fa real" in our lives — all the way!

To Love Means to Give

The Holy Spirit empowers us to make a sincere gift of ourselves. To love means to give.

When God loved the world so much, what did He do? He "*gave* his only Son" (Jn. 3:16).

That's why JP could say, in his encyclical on the mercy of God, "He who loves desires to give himself."

So love is at the heart of community. If to love means to give, what does that mean? Community lovin is goin to involve all kinds of givin.

TIME OUT! Check this out:

7 Ways to Give Yourself 2 Community Livin

1. Forgivin: *The most necessary!*
2. Givin in: *Obedience, the most difficult.*
3. Givin up: Sacrifice, *the greatest proof of our lovin (check out 1 John 3:16).*
4. Givin away: *This is pleasin to God (check out Acts 20:35 and 2 Corinthians 9:7).*
5. Almsgivin: *The most practical.*
6. Thanksgivin: *The best kind of givin.*
7. Life givin: *The greatest kind of givin.*

Great Expectations!

When JP was at the real "thrilla-in-Manila" — World Youth Day 1995, in the Philippines (they stopped countin after five million, the largest recorded gatherin in human history) — he responded to a question presented to him by the youth. JP gets personal:

You ask, "What are my expectations of young people?" In *Crossing The Threshold of Hope* I have written that "the fundamental problem of youth is profoundly personal. Young people . . . know that their life has meaning to the extent that it becomes a free gift for others." A question is therefore directed to each one of you personally: Are you capable of giving of yourself, your time, your energies, your talents, for the good of others? Are you capable of love? If you are, the Church and society can expect great things from each one of you.

What the Holy Father is doin here is challengin you to belong and confirmin that he wants you to belong, and that you do belong to Christ, to the Church, and to those who believe and live the abundant life in Christ! You do belong, but I know you don't always feel that you belong. Many times you aren't made to feel that you belong — sometimes this is done by people who are supposed to make you feel that you belong! That's alright! It's all good!

What's it mean "to belong" anyhow? It means to be in a proper situation, to be attached, to be connected, to be in a close, intimate relationship. It's all about belongin to Jesus.

Check out the way "belong" is used in the Scriptures:

1. Paul tells us we "belong" to Christ (Romans 1:6).
2. Paul says that dead or alive we "belong" to Him (Romans 14:8).
3. We "belong" to the light (1 Thessalonians 5:8-11).
4. We should do good to all, but especially to those who "belong" to the family of believers (Galatians 6:10).

Check it out: If U BELIEVE, U BELONG! Therefore, say with me, "I BELIEVE, THEREFORE I BELONG! AMEN!"
Say it even if you don't believe you belong! This will help you to believe!

This has got to become the "international anthem" for the civilization of love: "I believe, therefore I belong." St. Paul put it like this:

> So let no one boast about human leaders. For all things are yours, whether Paul or Apollos or Cephas or the world or life or death or the present or the future — all belong to you, and you belong to Christ, and Christ belongs to God. (1 Corinthians 3:21-23)

Got 2 Belong!

I'm sure you might have some good reasons for feelin that you don't belong in the Church, your family, your school, and even with some of your friends. I bet your reasons are pretty good reasons too — but they're not good enough!

You might be comparin yourself and your experiences to other people and their experiences: "I don't look like this." "I can't do that." "I don't have this" — or whatever! Your gut might be ragin with "I don't belong!"

U got 2 believe it! U got 2 read it! Open up your Bible and check this out:

➡ 1 Corinthians 12:12-31

Also check out:

➡ Ephesians 4:1-16

Christ's Body is one with many parts.

If we could just get this part a little bit better — to forget about ourselves in order to love others — we'd all be feelin a whole lot more of the unity of community! We would have the feelin and give the feelin to others: "I belong! You belong! We belong!"

Man, just think about the extremes that people go through just to have a sense of "I belong." That's what's up with gangs. People in gangs want and get (wrongly) a strong sense of "I belong." It's part of the stupidity and absurdity of the modern age to think that we can have a sense of "I belong" without sacrifice. No way! Got to have sacrifice!

Look at what gang members go through, and members of some college fraternities go through, in order to belong. Take a look at some of the dumb things you may have done in order to have that sense of "I belong." This is huge, dude!

I know a junior high school kid in the South Bronx who put a weapon to another kid's throat in order to belong. His father is not in his life, so there is a huge daddy boo-boo here! He's missin his daddy, and he's desperate for his father's presence and love in his life. As a result, anything goes as long as he doesn't have to feel the pain and can feel that he belongs somehow, somewhere, to somebody! Know what I'm sayin?

Look at all the problems and how much pain is caused when people are made to feel that they don't belong. It goes deep.

Not Belongin?

I've been all over the world, seen all kinds of communities, rich and poor. Let me tell ya: It's everywhere! Sometimes people think about takin their own life. Sometimes they try to take their own life, and thank God they don't succeed. Sometimes someone tragically succeeds in taking their own life. Lord, have mercy — and He does.

This is all goin on right now as I'm writin this and as you're readin it. So let's stop and pray for our brothers and sisters, young and old, who are really desperate and sufferin, with no hope, whose hearts are crushed.

Lord Jesus, please come to the rescue of our brothers and sisters who at this moment are really

strugglin cause they feel they don't belong and want out. Turn them around, Lord, and turn on the light in their hearts. Be with them and their families and their friends.

Also, Lord, for those who have taken their own lives, we pray for them and their families and their friends. May they rest in your peace. Amen.

Hail Mary, full of grace, the Lord is with thee. Blessed art thou amongst women, and blessed is the fruit of thy womb, Jesus. Holy Mary, Mother of God, pray for us sinners, now and at the hour of our death. Amen.

I wrote a song about not belongin and havin no hope. It is a rewrite of the old school song "Kumbya, My Lord." I included "Kumbya (Pass By My Way)" on my Sacro Song CD. Check it out:

You think it's you against the world feelin low gettin high,
With supposed friends smokin dope — no hope.
Drug dealin thug money livin life on a tightrope,
Dial a psychic every day read the horoscope.
Feelin low can't say no — can't cope.
What if I did it with my little sister's jump rope?
My heart's in pain it hits me hard with a KO.
Can't sleep I'm havin visions of a death blow.
Memories from long ago . . . Lord help me I can't let 'em go.
Where's my friends? I feel lonely with no advocate.
I feel unimportant so inadequate.
Will I ever find a way to get out of it?
Bad feelins gettin strong gettin way too passionate.
I'm losin ground I'm getin real desperate.
Don't wanna act in a way that's inappropriate.
I shut down . . . run away in isolation.
Somebody help me I can use some affirmation.
I'm tellin you the truth I got no time for fabrication.

Don't know who I am what's up with my vocation?
I feel like I'm damned with no hope for salvation.
No matter what I do I seem to get aggravation.
I got no one I can trust nobody to confide.
Life is hard I feel dissatisfied.
I got too much pride to pay for a homicide.
I'm afraid of heights can't jump the mountain side.
Don't wanna get bug-eyed and drink pesticide.
Got no car can't poison me with carbon monoxide.
I'm feelin so confused it's a bad time to decide.
Can't help the way I feel my mind is so preoccupied.
Forget about a shotgun forget about suicide.
Get lucky cross the street end it with a hit-and-run.
Times are bad will the Son finally come?
Get taken out with the coming of the third millennium.
Can I eat a stray bullet kill me with a ricochet.
Too much pain . . . How can I break away?
Can somebody teach me?
Can somebody teach me how to pray?
Stop all the hoopla . . . Kyrie.
Open up my heart there's a lot of things I gotta say.
Kumbya my Lord, pass by my way.
Open up my heart there's a lot of things I gotta say.
Kumbya my Lord, pass by my way.
It's the only way I overcome everything every day.

How Do You Spell *Church?* I Belong!

Jesus founded the Church.

Jesus founded the Church to which we all can belong and make everyone feel that they belong. That's why when He taught us to pray, He taught us to say "Our Father" — not "my Father" or "your Father," but "Our Father." That makes us all brothers and sisters, with no exception. We belong to one another. We are one body. We are family.

This doesn't mean that everybody has to join your parish and get listed on the envelope system. But it does mean that we have to love and make people feel they belong as a brother or sister who is loved and respected and cared for. Check out CCC #1658 if you think I'm foolin. The Church teaches that no one is an orphan since it is a home and family for everyone!

By the way, if folks had a bigger sense of "I belong," our parishes would see bigger improvements in the collection! Bigger improvements in singin and bein involved. More life! More love! More community!

Time to Get Busy!

Come on! Let's get busy! No mo feelin sorry for ourselves and waitin for somebody else to make you feel you belong.

You do belong. U got 2 believe.

Go and make somebody else feel they belong and you'll experience belongin like never before! Now we can have a better feel for why the Church understands her deepest vocation to be communion — F.A.M.I.L.Y.

Communion means to share, to have intimate fellowship, to live and love together as a community, givin others the sense that they belong. Communion is the vocation of the family of God (check out CCC #959). This means, in theory, that everybody belongs. This theory is truth — and this truth must be practiced and lived out every day. The truth will set you free, set me free, set us free! We got 2 B free!

How Do We Do Dat?

We've got to develop and promote a spirituality of communion — this is F.A.M.I.L.Y. big time! JP says we've got to make the Church the home and the school of communion: "That is the greatest challenge facing us in the millennium which is now beginning, if we wish to be faithful to God's plan and respond to the world's deepest yearnings" (*Novo Millennio Ineunte* #43).

The Pope wants us to get this goin wherever families and communities are bein built up. He gives us four points to help us do it. Let me break it down 4 U:

1. First, we need to pray and contemplate the mystery of the Trinity dwelling within us. This will enable us to see the light of the Trinity "shining on the face of the brothers and sisters around us" (*Novo Millennio Ineunte* #43).

2. Secondly, we need to develop the ability to think of our brothers and sisters in the Mystical Body of Christ as " 'those who are a part of me.' This makes us able to share their joys and sufferings, to sense their desires and attend to their needs, to offer them deep and genuine friendship" (*Novo Millennio Ineunte* #43).

3. Thirdly, we need to develop the ability to see what is positive in others, "to welcome it and prize it as a gift from God: not only as a gift for the brother or sister who has received it directly, but also as a 'gift for me' " (*Novo Millennio Ineunte* #43).

4. Finally, we need "to know how to 'make room' for our brothers and sisters, bearing 'each other's burdens' (Gal 6:2) and resisting the selfish temptations which constantly beset us and provoke competition, careerism, distrust and jealousy" (*Novo Millennio Ineunte* #43).

Keepin It Real

Doesn't it sound good on paper? The Church is the Body of Christ, and there's room for everybody in Jesus! We got 2 make room. We got 2 believe!

What are we doin to make a difference? How do we hold up when inconvenience shows up and demands of us a sacrifice? How is your parish more lively and lovin, more of a home and family for others because of you? Do you feel you belong? What are you doin to make others feel that they belong? Remember, F.A.M.I.L.Y. means "Forget about me, I love you," not "Forget about you, I love me!" Watch out!

You might be sayin, "Dis sounds good, Fadda, but I don't feel at home in my parish, so how can I make others feel at home?"

F.A.M.I.L.Y. Forget about how you feel for a moment and think about how many other people might feel the same way you do!

When you think how unwelcome and "not at home" they may feel, why not pray for the amazin grace of courage? Courage will give you the mental toughness to overcome the fear and danger of bein rejected and thought of as a fool by others. Who cares what anybody thinks as long as you're tryin to do the right thing! (Right thing = Will of God!)

Think about if all the people who feel unwelcome start makin others feel welcome. There's gonna be a whole bunch of welcomed people! See what I'm sayin?

So if there're no opportunities for something like this in your parish, connect with some folks who feel the same way you do, and who are willin to commit to make a difference, and go have a chat with your pastor. And if that doesn't work, go to the bishop!

You can tell your pastor — and the bishop, if necessary — that the Pope wants you involved. He doesn't want you to grow lax. Are you ready for some of that? Now were talkin bout community!

Check out what JP said at World Youth Day 2000 in Rome:

When you return home, do not grow lax. *["Lax" means to be soft, loose, not strong; to weaken, like lettin the fire die out.]* Reinforce and deepen your bond with the Christian communities to which you belong. From Rome, from the City of Peter and Paul, the Pope follows you with affection and, paraphrasing St. Catherine of Siena's words, reminds you: "If you are what you should be, you will set the whole world ablaze!"

So before y'all set the whole world on fire, how about startin with your parish?

But remember, you and I don't have the power to do this or something like it. We need Jesus, the Holy Spirit, the Blessed Mother, and all the help we can get! Remember, we belong to Him! The world community needs Jesus. This includes your immediate family as well as your parish family. With the great gift of Jesus in the Eucharist, we can be energized to make the best choices we can to build community.

Let's go to JP at World Youth Day in Rome one mo time:

> The world must not be deprived of the gentle and liberating presence of Christ living in the Eucharist! You yourselves must be fervent witnesses to Christ's presence on the altar. Let the Eucharist mold your life and the life of the families you will form. Let it guide all life's choices.

The Pope's Countin on U

JP's countin on you to form communities — in your school, in the street, with your friends, at home, in your parishes, as well as with the families you will form from your flesh if you marry and God blesses you with children someday. Even if some of you become priests, deacons, or consecrated brothers and sisters, the same is true for you.

The Holy Father is countin on you to let the Eucharist mold your lives. This is how you can get the job done and be saved from the curse of sittin back and waitin for somebody else to do it. As the old sayin goes, "If not you, who? If not now, when?"

You got to contribute to buildin community whatever your personal vocation may be. This is so because, as we have seen with communion, buildin community is the deepest vocation of the Church.

The Pope expects it from you. He's waitin for you to get it goin with Jesus, to be more and more like Jesus! As he said in his encyclical on the Gospel of Life, "To give his life is the real object of Jesus' mission: he is the one who 'comes down from heaven, and gives life to the world' (Jn. 6:33)' " (*Evangelium Vitae* #37). R U willin to increase the donation of yourself?

Take a Stand for Jesus — Go Against the Flow

Are you willing to make the necessary sacrifices and take a stand for Jesus? It's a must if we are to follow Jesus. It's what JP calls a "new martyrdom."

In case you don't know, a "martyr" is someone who witnessed the truth of the faith to the point of death. The word *martyr* literally means "witness." Think about bein sworn in to testify to the whole truth and nothin but the truth so help U God! You'll get the picture.

The martyrs of the past testified to the truth of Jesus by dyin for Him, rather than renouncin Him.

Lookin back again at World Youth Day 2000, Pope John Paul II said, "To follow Jesus . . . demands of us, just as it did in the past, that we take a stand for him, almost to the point at times of a new martyrdom: the martyrdom of those who, today as yesterday, are called to go against the tide in order to follow the divine Master."

JP is givin it to us straight, as is his custom! To go against the tide, to go against the flow — the flow and energy of the culture of death! It's everywhere! That's why he wants us to work at buildin up the civilization of love! That's how he talks about community, and he has a lot to say about it — and we got to check it out.

A New Humanity

As we let the Eucharist form and reform our lives, we will be able to take that firm stand for Jesus that JP was talkin about. This will have tremendous results! It will give rise to a "new humanity." That's pretty deep and awesome.

Currently, there's not much respect for anything in our culture. There is a lack of respect for ourselves, for others, for the sacredness of our bodies — a lack of respect for the un-born, newborn, and the old-born! We got to change that! U got 2 believe!

The Holy Father is lookin forward to a radical change to all of this and is countin on you to make the difference.

(I hope you don't mind me speakin out on his behalf: I'm the self-appointed, unofficial Vatican ambassador of the Holy Father, Pope John Paul II. If it's the only way I can get to see him, I'm prayin somebody reports me to the Vatican so I can be called in for a "personal" reprimand! Alleluia!)

The Pope has said — again, during World Youth Day 2000 in Rome — "I look forward to this new humanity that you are helping to prepare. I look to this Church that in every age is made youthful by the Spirit of Christ and today is made happy by your intentions and commitment." JP calls this "new hu-manity" the "civilization of love." He's an awesome witness to it too! Will you join him? Let's do it!

The Civilization of Love

The most important dimension of the civilization of love is the same thing that energizes F.A.M.I.L.Y. — forgettin about yourself and lovin the other by makin a gift of yourself for the other. It ain't all about what you can get, but what you can give.

So the next time you say or hear, "I don't get anything out of church," you got to ask: "What are you givin?"

I'm not talkin bout your money either, even though we got to do that too. Remember what I said earlier on about how we got to have a self that is loved in the first place before we can forget about it and give it away. You can't give what you don't have!

Check out what JP says is the most important dimension of the civilization of love. It's the "radical acceptance of the understanding of man as a person who 'finds himself' by mak-ing a sincere gift of self. A gift is, obviously, 'for others': this is *the most important dimension* of the civilization of love" (Letter to Families #14).

What's bein said here is a key teachin to the life and ministry of Pope John Paul II. It's at the heart of the Gospel, and it's at the heart of community.

Remember this: **GS 24**. It's an abbreviation for *Gaudium et Spes* — a little Latin here. In English, it's known as the Pastoral Constitution on the Church in the Modern World — a very important document from the famous Second Vatican Council.

Say it again: **GS 24**. It's a favorite of JP's, and that means it's gonna be a favorite of mine! Here goes!

The basic teachin of GS 24 is given in a two-punch combo: kinda like Scripture and Tradition — jab, jab, jab with Tradition, and then throw the knockout punch with Scripture! Same here: jab, jab, jab with Part One of GS 24: "Man . . . is the only creature on earth which God willed for itself." We are special!

In commentin on this, JP said, "God hands man over to himself, entrusting him both to his family and to society as their responsibility" (Letter to Families, #9).

Now comes Part Two of GS 24, the knockout punch: "Man . . . cannot fully find himself except through a sincere gift of himself." Boom! The knockout punch for all selfishness, egoism, materialism, secularism — and the culture of death itself!

This is the victory plan for the buildin up of the civilization of love — the real-deal community! It's the inner logic of F.A.M.I.L.Y.

This is love lived out: "Love causes man to find fulfillment through the sincere gift of self. To love means to give and to receive something which can be neither bought nor sold, but only given freely and mutually" (Letter to Families, #11).

In his book *Crossing the Threshold of Hope*, the Pope said it again: "Man affirms himself most completely by giving himself. This is the fulfillment of the commandment of love (Gal. 5:13-15)."

Its kinda like this: The more we give of ourselves, the happier we will be and the more joy we will share. Maybe that's why there are so many unhappy people in the world community today — the Church included! Not enough sincere givin of self will result in a lot of sad people.

We Shall Be Judged

Community is spelled F.A.M.I.L.Y., and family is all about love, and we better get this love thing together because that's what it's all about. We will be judged on love. I know y'all wanna make it to the "Kingdom" family reunion, right?

In his Letter to Families, Pope John Paul II quotes St. John of the Cross, one of his favorite writers: "In the evening of life we shall be judged on love" (Letter to Families, #22). In other words, when we die, we will be judged on how much we loved. Love kept the saints marchin on in this world, and love got the saints marchin on in the world to come. Do you want to be among that number, among the great cloud of witnesses?

TIME OUT! Boy, does John Paul II love saints! He's canonized more saints and beatified more blesseds than all the popes of the twentieth century combined! Check out these old and incomplete statistics:

- All the popes of the twentieth century: 158 saints and 79 blesseds.
- JP so far: 451 saints and 1,220 blesseds!

Alleluia!

Every man and woman fully realizes himself or herself through a sincere gift of self. In meditatin on this key teachin of GS 24, in light of the great judgment of MT 25 (that's Matthew 25), the Holy Father gives us a glimpse of what the civilization of love looks like. Check out the great heart of JP. Talk about a two-punch combo: GS 24 and MT 25: " 'I was an unborn child, and you welcomed me by letting me be born'; 'I was an abandoned child, and you became my family'; 'I was an orphan, and you adopted me and raised me as one of your own children.' Or again: 'You helped mothers filled with uncertainty and exposed to wrongful pressure to welcome their unborn child and let it be born'; and 'You helped large families and families in difficulty to look after and educate the children God gave them" (Letter to Families, #22).

Alleluia! Now that's F.A.M.I.L.Y.!

More With Us Than There Are With Them

This community-and-communion thing is huge! It's not just "here," but "up there" — in heaven.

Meditatin with JP helps us to realize this. Remember how Jesus taught us how to pray: "Our Father, who art in heaven, hallowed be thy name; thy kingdom come, thy will be done on earth as it is in heaven."

The community of heaven is to help the community on earth! Jesus wants us to pray about doin God's will on earth "as it is in heaven" because He wants us to do God's will on earth "as it is in heaven"!

The Church teaches that the earthly and heavenly cities, communities, or families have a way of relating with each other. Sometimes we forget that. Remember, we are never alone in this fight. We got lots of help!

Open up your Bible and check this out:

➥ 2 Kings 6:8-23

There are more of us than there are of them.

In the Second Book of Kings, there is the story of Elisha bein surrounded by his enemies, the Arameans. When Elisha's servant sees that they are surrounded by the mighty armies, he runs to Elisha in fear. We can learn a lot from Elisha's response: "Do not be afraid, for there are more with us than there are with them" (2 Kings 5:20).

Elisha then prays that God will open the eyes of his servant so that he might see what he means by this, and the Scriptures tell us, "So the LORD opened the eyes of the servant, and he saw; the mountain was full of horses and chariots of fire all around Elisha" (2 Kings 5:17).

We got the power of God, and we got the community of believers, both those who are livin in this world and those in the next, supportin us. God's angels are there to help us too.

We don't have to feel alone, even when by all appearances it seems that we are. Pray that God will open your eyes to see the bigger picture! You and I have friends in high places. Know what I'm sayin?

Friends

Friends are really important for life and community, and they are a beautiful gift from God. The same is true with friends "up there" — the saints: St. Frances and St. Clare, St. Ephrem (They call him the "Harp of the Holy Spirit." I was born on his feast day. He's totally cool: Doctor of the Church, mystic, contemplative, social activist caring for the poor, poet, author, and inspired musician — and a great saint!), St. Teresa of Ávila (I like to call her "Big T"), St. Thérèse of Lisieux (I like to call her "Little T." Most folks call her "The Little Flower" — she's my "little wild flower"!), St. Anthony . . . I have lots more and could do a whole book on the saints!

Do you have a favorite saint? Have you ever checked em out? Find a good book, or get on the Internet and do a search for saints and your patron saint. Most folks are named after a saint. If you're not, ask the Lord to hook you up with a new friend. What a blessin!

There's a really cool thing called "the communion of saints." This is another one of those really "Catholic" things. It's crucial for a Catholic sense of community. Lots of folks — Catholics and non-Catholics alike — don't understand what we do. Pray to saints?

Don't you talk to your friends and ask them to pray for you? Sure you do! So let's do a little "on earth as it is in heaven" here! If we talk to our friends "down here," have pictures of them, and ask them to pray for us, why not do the same with our friends "up there"?

Friends have a critical role to play in community. We're so influenced by the people we hang with. Spendin time with people definitely influences how we think, feel, and make decisions. Followin somebody's example is one of the great things about the saints! It all starts with Jesus. Is He your best friend? Think about it.

I Ain't Worshipin No Saints

Amen!

St. Paul said, "Be imitators of me, as I am of Christ" (1 Corinthians 11:1). Imitation is the key for our veneration of the saints and is very biblical for all of you who are worried bout that.

Veneration ain't worship. Worship is for God alone. Veneration is nothin more than respect or awe inspired by the dignity, wisdom, dedication , talent, and holiness of a person.

Check out what St. Paul says to the Philippians in 3:17: "Brothers and sisters, join in imitating me, and observe those who live according to the example you have in us."

Now maybe you can see why JP has said, "It is important to know the personalities and spiritualities of our saints, so as to be able to imitate them in the life of grace and testimony and call upon them at moments of bewilderment and temptation."

Read this:

Catechism of the Catholic Church ➡ #957

The Church's teaching on the communion of saints.

U Don't Have 2 Wait!

One of my good friends, St. Isaac of Syria, puts it like this: "The path of God is a daily cross. No one has ascended into heaven by means of ease, for we know where the way of ease leads and how it ends." Don't wanna end up there! Know what I'm sayin?

So we don't have to wait until we die till we can experience a taste of the final state of heaven — and thanks be to God for that! It can be anticipated right here, right now! Check out JP again on the final state of heaven, given during a general audience, July 21, 1999:

> This final state . . . can be anticipated in some way today in sacramental life, whose center is the Eucharist, and in the gift of self through fraternal charity. If we are able to enjoy properly the good things that the Lord showers upon us every day, we will already have begun to experience that joy and peace which one day will be completely ours. We know that on this earth everything is subject to limits, but the thought of the "ultimate" realities helps us to live better the "penultimate" [in other words, "next to last"] realities.

He Wants Us to Be Saints!

Pope John Paul II is callin you to be a saint of the new millennium, a saint of the new humanity, a saint of the new evangelization, a saint of the new community — a saint of the civilization of love!

"Who me"?

You got it!

"But I'm afraid."

What do you think JP is gonna say to you? Four of his favorite words: "Do not be afraid."

Check out what the Pope has to say to you (from a talk given during World Youth Day, June 29, 1999):

Young people of every continent, do not be afraid to be the saints of the new millennium! Be contemplative, love prayer; be coherent with your faith *[be clear about it and understand it; be consistent with it and make it part of your daily life]* and generous in the service of your brothers and sisters; be active members of the Church and builders of peace. To succeed in this demanding project of life, continue to listen to his Word, draw strength from the sacraments, especially the Eucharist and Penance. The Lord wants you to be intrepid apostles *[to be characterized by fearlessness, strength, and endurance]* of his Gospel and builders of a new humanity. In fact, how can you say you believe in God made man without taking a firm position against all that destroys the human person and the family? If you believe that Christ has revealed the Father's love for every person, you cannot fail to strive to contribute to the building of a new world, founded on the power of love and forgiveness, on the struggle against injustice and all physical, moral and spiritual distress, on the orientation of politics, economy, culture and technology to the service of man and his integral development. . . . May Most Holy Mary teach you, dear young people, how to discern the will of the heavenly Father in your life.

A Very Special Intercessor — the Blessed Virgin Mary

If community is spelled F.A.M.I.L.Y. (and it is), and if God is our Father (and He is), and if we have friends in high places (and we do), then we can see why Mary is our mother — and thanks be to God she is!

Lots of folks don't click with the Blessed Mother. Some folks don't even like her, which I can't understand. But check it out: If you can't click with her or like her, you at lease got to respect her. If you're not respectin her, you're disrespectin her.

Talk about "on earth as it is in heaven"!

Try disrespectin somebody's mother here on earth. You're in for trouble. How could somebody down here even think about disrespectin Somebody's mother "up there"?

They're probably not thinkin at all, and could be in for some serious, big-time trouble! Especially when that "Somebody" is Jesus, the King of the Universe, the Lord of lords, the King of Heaven? Not a good idea.

Like I said, if you don't like Mary, that's you — but you got to at least respect her. Jesus is God. Mary is the mother of Jesus. Mary is the Mother of God. Case closed.

Think of what a family is like with a great mom? Just think of what a family is like with a heavenly mother? Think of what a family is like without a mom. Not a good scene.

Or what's a family like with a mom who is really strugglin and for whatever reason hasn't been, and can't be, a good mom? Not a good scene — and we have plenty of em. Mary can help us love Jesus as no one else can.

Jesus is the King, and Mary is the Queen. Jesus is the Rock, and Mary is the mother of the Rock! As our heavenly mother, she's been given some awesome gifts by our heavenly Father. She's been given the greatest gift of all, Jesus Christ in the flesh, in her blessed womb. She can help us so much. Give her a chance and she'll give you her Son, and you'll have everything you need.

If anybody thinks that Mary "takes away" from Jesus, think again. The Church teaches that Mary's role in the Church cannot be separated from her relationship with Christ. In the *Catechism*, the Church teaches that " 'Mary's function as mother of men in no way obscures or diminishes this unique mediation of Christ, but rather shows it its power. But the Blessed Virgin's salutary influence on men . . . flows forth from the superabundance of the merits of Christ, rests on his mediation, depends entirely on it, and draws all its power from it' " (CCC #970).

Amen!

Let's pray with JP, who has a very special love for our Blessed Virgin Mary, Mother of God, Mother of the Church, Mother of all communities and families:

May the Virgin Mary help us to open the doors of our hearts to Christ, Redeemer of man and of history; may she teach us to be humble, because God looks upon the lowly; may she enable us to grow in understanding the value of prayer, of inner silence, of listening to God's Word; may she spur us to seek God's will deeply and sincerely, even when this upsets our plans; may she encourage us while we wait for the Lord, sharing our time and energy with those in need.

Amen!

But whenever you pray, go into your room and shut the door and pray to your Father who is in secret; and your Father who sees in secret will reward you.

Matthew 6:6

CHAPTER 6

Prayer: U Got 2 Do It!

Talkin to God: Thirty-three Considerations on Prayer

Prayer is a very personal thing. It's somethin U got 2 do.

Jesus tells us to go to our room, shut the door, and pray to our Father who sees in secret and He will reward us. How you pray is one thing; that you actually pray *is the thing*. Jesus keeps it very simple. My intention here is to do the same — to keep it simple.

I'm presentin the following thirty-three considerations on prayer as a manual. I'm gonna lay out stuff to you in a way that will hopefully help you to pray. A manual is a book that is "conveniently handled." These considerations do not have to be read in order. Just read em.

Hopefully, somethin here will help you to pray. It ain't all about understandin it right now, but it is all about just doin it. (To get a lifetime understandin of prayer, be sure to read the last, the shortest, and the best part in the *Catechism of the Catholic Church* — Part Four: Christian Prayer, #2558-2865).

Consideration #1

You will be rewarded if you pray. You might not get what you want when you want it, but you will be rewarded. Jesus promised that when you pray, "your Father who sees in secret will reward you." So pray and put your trust in God. Talk to Him. Tell Him what's goin on or not goin on. Tell God how you feel. Make known your needs. Pray for your friends, your family, the lonely, the sick and dying, the poor, the Church, and the world.

TIME OUT! In case you feel uncomfortable with this "reward thing," check out my favorite theologian, Hans Urs von Balthasar, in his book The Grain of Wheat:

It can be arrogance not to accept God's rewards and promises . . . it can equally be selfish to want to serve God on account of this reward, to want to become rich "off him." We escape the dilemma if we consider that our reward is God, that God is love and love does not look to itself, much less to a reward.

Consideration #2

You might be sayin, "I don't know how to pray."

I say, "Pray anyhow!" That means pray any way you can, even though you think and feel you don't know how. You can still do it. Jesus keeps it very simple. Go to your room and close the door.

"I don't have my own room."

So go somewhere for a little while where you can be somewhat alone and talk to God. U got 2 believe! U got 2 do it! Don't tell me you don't know how to pray. Tell Him. That's a great prayer right there. Congratulations!

Consideration #3

The Bible tells us in 1 Peter 4:7 to remain calm so that we can pray. It doesn't say pray to remain calm. Don't get me wrong. It's great and necessary to ask God to calm us down. He will. That's not the point.

The point is that it's important to prepare ourselves somehow before we spend "quality time" with God.

Don't just talk to Him. Listen to Him and just be there. This is a discipline thing. It takes some gettin used to.

Consideration #4

"What kinda stuff can I do to spend some quality time with God?" It doesn't take much. Keep it simple.

TIME OUT! Check out the Capuchin Poor Clare nun Bl. Angela Maria Astorch:

It's enough for me to hear a bird sing, to smell the fragrance of a flower, to listen to music *[Come on, Sista!]*, to hear the sound of bells or the peal of thunder or some passage from the Gospel or the Psalms, and then I feel such a touch of the divine in my inmost being that my heart awakens and becomes light, light as if it possessed wings to lift it up to its true homeland.

Consideration #5

Pray as you can, not as you can't. So if you're really tired, don't try to pray for a long time. Pray — but pray for a short time. You'll fall right to sleep! And what a great way to fall asleep — prayin!

But you want to be fresh and at your best for the Lord. So when you plan to pray for a little longer stretch of time, take a nap first so you can give your best to God. The Lord usually gets the short end of the stick when it comes to us bein with Him, when it comes to prayer. Try not to make this the case in your life!

Consideration #6

U got 2 have a regular place to pray, to be with the Lord.

I have a "prayer spot" in my room — with my crucifix, candle, and an icon of the Blessed Mother. It helps me to focus, even as I walk in and out of my room.

If you don't have the luxury of your own room, if you share a room and there's no space, make a "prayer pack" and put it in a plastic bag, a shoppin bag, a special prayer bag, or any kinda bag for the road or wherever you can make a temporary spot to pray. Crucifix, Bible, rosary, candle (be careful with candles; you can't always use'em) — pack em up and pray!

It's the effort here that will be your biggest blessin. Don't sweat not havin the "perfect situation." There ain't one this side of heaven. Make the effort and pray — otherwise, you never will.

Consideration #7

Know that it's always possible to pray.

No matter what's goin on or where we are, we can always pray. Jesus is always with us. St John Chrysostom said, "It is possible to offer fervent prayer even while walking in public, or strolling alone, or seated in your shop . . . while buying or selling . . . or even while cooking."

Sounds like St. John had "been there — done that." U and I got 2 do it 2!

Consideration #8

We will not be able to pray well at any time, anywhere, if we do not pray at a specific time in a specific place. U got 2 have a routine.

Mornin is my best time to pray. I get up early cause once the day gets rollin, fa-get-a-bout-it.

Check out what the Church says about it: "We cannot pray 'at all times' if we do not pray at specific times, consciously willing it" (CCC #2697).

Consideration #9

We got to have the will to pray.

"Prayer cannot be reduced to the spontaneous outpouring of interior impulse: in order to pray, one must have the will to pray. Nor is it enough to know what the Scriptures reveal about prayer: one must also learn how to pray" (CCC #2650).

Consideration #10

We got to learn how to pray from our great tradition on prayer. There are so many people with lots of experience at prayin. Don't focus on your lack of experience. Focus on the Lord and on those to whom He has given great gifts and experiences of prayer.

"The tradition of Christian prayer is one of the ways in which the tradition of faith takes shape and grows, especially through the contemplation and study of believers who treasure in their hearts the events and words of the economy of salvation, and through their profound grasp of the spiritual realities they experience" (CCC #2651).

Consideration #11

According to the experience of "Little T" — St. Thérèse of Lisieux — prayer is really simple, and it helped her deal with good and bad times. She says, "For me, prayer is a surge of the heart; it is a simple look turned toward heaven, it is a cry of recognition and of love, embracing both trial and joy" (CCC #2558).

Consideration #12

The more we pray, the more we grow in inner freedom and confidence during trials.

"As Christian experience attests especially in prayer, the more docile we are to the promptings of grace, the more we grow in inner freedom and confidence during trials, such as those we face in the pressures and constraints of the outer world. By the working of grace the Holy Spirit educates us in spiritual freedom in order to make us free collaborators in his work in the Church and in the world" (CCC #1742).

Consideration #13

It's crucial to pray for, and to pray with, our families. Durin the Year of the Family (1994), Pope John Paul II said, "Prayer must become the dominant element of the Year of the Family in the Church: prayer by the family, prayer for the family, and prayer with the family."

Have you ever prayed with your immediate family or with a family member, apart from going to Mass? Maybe a decade of the Rosary together? Maybe one Our Father, a Hail Mary, and a Glory be? What about givin it a try?

Consideration #14

According to St. Francis de Sales, there are three necessary conditions for prayer:

1. Be little by humility.
2. Be great in hope.
3. Be grafted onto Jesus Christ crucified.

Consideration #15

Don't be afraid to try to plan once in a while, for starters, to pray for a little bit longer time than you're used to.

What's a long time? An hour, or simply just a little bit more time than what you're used to.

What's it like to pray for a long time? Find out for yourself!

Consideration #16

"How can I hear God speak to me as I spend time with
Him in prayer?"

Be faithful and keep prayin. Somethin will happen! Ya never
know where, when, or how.

God is not limited to speak to you when you want Him to
or expect Him to. When you pray to hear His voice, give Him
permission to speak to you wherever, whenever, and however
He pleases. You just may be surprised!

Consideration #17

Do you ask God to bless you and the food you are about to eat when you're out in public with your friends at the local pizza place or hamburger joint — even just makin the Sign of the Cross with your head bowed and no words?

Body prayer!

Consideration #18

Do you pray with your friends when you get together to hang out, play sports, go to the movies, travel by car, or go on a date?

It might sound kinda weird, especially if you're not used to prayin a whole bunch. But once you get over the initial "embarrassment," you'll be fine.

Sometimes it's hard to pray with others when all is goin well. But if there's some kinda big problem, the prayer kinda just flows. Don't wait for a tragedy to lead you to prayer. Get there first! All shall be well. U got 2 pray!

Consideration #19

Do you pray with the community at Mass by sayin the responses and acclamations with wide-open mouth and all your heart? Or is your public prayer "lukewarm," closed-mouthed, mumbled, half-hearted, and passionless?

The great and awesome prayer of the Mass is a wonderful opportunity for us to prayerfully and passionately proclaim our faith.

Consideration #20

St. Augustine said, "When you sing, you pray twice."

Singin is a powerful form of prayer. Try singin to God alone, listenin to someone else sing to God, or singin to God with others as you worship at Mass or at any time. It's an awesome experience.

"But I can't sing." Sing anyway, and offer your heart to God as you sing.

Consideration #21

To become comfortable with singin God's praises is to become comfortable with the language of heaven, our true home.

Check out what my hero, John Paul II, said in St. Louis in 1999:
Our true mother tongue is the praise of God, the language of heaven, our true home. . . . As we look at the century we are leaving behind, we see that human pride and the power of sin have made it difficult for many people to speak their mother tongue. In order to be able to sing God's praises we must relearn the language of humility and trust, the language of moral integrity and of sincere commitment to all that is truly good in the sight of the Lord.

Consideration #22

Praise is somethin most Catholics are not used to doin outside of Mass. It's an awesome form of prayer.

The Holy Spirit can free our minds, hearts, and tongues to praise God. "Praise is the form of prayer which recognizes most immediately that God is God. It lauds God for his own sake and gives him glory, quite beyond what he does, but simply because HE IS" (CCC #2639).

Consideration #23

Prayer can be expressed through worship, praise, and song. These different forms of prayer help us to believe and understand the great mystery of faith.

> TIME OUT! *Check out Rabbi Abraham Heschel, from his book* Moral Grandeur and Spiritual Audacity:
>
> The beginning of prayer is praise. The power of worship is song. First we sing, then we understand. First we praise, then we believe. Praise and song open eyes to the grandeur of reality that transcends the self. Song restores the soul; praise repairs spiritual deficiency.

Consideration #24

Sometimes a sigh can be a powerful form of prayer. This can be very helpful, especially when you're frustrated and overwhelmed, feelin like ya just don't know how to pray. Don't despair!

The Holy Spirit helps us in our weakness. St. Paul says, "The Spirit helps us in our weakness; for we do not know how to pray as we ought, but that very Spirit intercedes with sighs too deep for words" (Romans 8:26).

This is a great way to pray with the Holy Spirit: Breathe the Holy Spirit in, and sigh all the garbage out.

Consideration #25

To be faithful to a life of prayer is gonna be a struggle. We have to make an effort. So don't be surprised if you find yourself havin to overcome all kinds of stuff within yourself — distractions, laziness, bein tired, doubts, inner dryness, and not havin enough time. Try to stay calm and keep prayin.

"Prayer presupposes an effort, a fight against ourselves and the wiles of the Tempter. The battle of prayer is inseparable from the necessary 'spiritual battle' to act habitually according to the Spirit of Christ: we pray as we live, because we live as we pray" (CCC #2752).

Consideration #26

If our prayer is to be pleasing to God, we got to be sure that it's accompanied by a positive difference in the way we live. In other words, we got to be growin in holiness.

> *TIME OUT! Read what Blessed Maria Magdalena Martinengo, a Capuchiness, had to say:*
>
> God is not pleased with prayers that are not accompanied by our perfection. Believe me, one act of virtue is worth any number of Rosaries. . . . What is the use of prayer if we do not emerge from it mortified, patient, humble, charitable, loving silence, willing to suffer, and to take on ourselves any kind of labor to help others?

Consideration #27

We have become so used to noise that silence makes most people feel really uncomfortable.

Silence is critical for a life of prayer, for a life committed to the Lord. Don't let the silence of the early dawn or the late night pass you by.

Wake up early (there is silence even in the South Bronx very early in the mornin!), stay up late, or make a short vigil by wakin up in the middle of the night to encounter the Lord in the silence.

It's true that we need to be well rested in order to pray well. God also blesses our efforts and can multiply hours when we sacrifice some of our time to Him for prayer, for silence.

Check out what Pope John Paul II says about the importance of silence:

Silence is the vital space dedicated to the Lord, in an atmosphere of listening and of assimilating his Word. . . . It is the sanctuary of prayer, the home of reflection and contemplation. To remain fervent and zealous in one's ministry, it is necessary to know how to receive the divine inspirations which come interiorly. And it is possible to do this only if one can spend time with the Divine Master. Jesus did not only call the Twelve that "he might send them forth to preach, and have authority over demons" but primarily so that "they might be with him" (Mk 3:14-15). . . . To be with Jesus: this should be your greatest desire. . . . To speak with him in a familiar way, to listen to him and follow him docilely: this is not only an understandable demand for whoever wants to follow the Lord; it is also an indispensable condition for all authentic and credible evangelization. He is an empty preacher of the Word, St. Augustine appropriately observes, who does not first listen to it himself. (*L'Osservatore Romano* [*that's the Vatican's newspaper*] March 25, 1992, p. 3)

Consideration #28

Prayer takes time.

Most of the time we don't have time to pray. We got to make time to pray. Even when time is on your side, you got to make that time for prayer.

It's a great help to know that the Holy Spirit "is offered to us at all times, in the events of *each day*, to make prayer spring up from us" (CCC #2659).

The issue of "I don't have time," therefore, doesn't become too much of an issue because of the Holy Spirit, who can make prayer spring up from us in the events of each day — if we let Him. That's a big "if." It becomes even much less of an issue if we give our time to Christ. That's the secret: Give your time to Jesus.

Check out what the Holy Father says about givin time to Jesus:

Do not be afraid to give your time to Christ! Yes, let us open our time to Christ, that he may cast light upon it and give it direction. He is the one who knows the secret of time and the secret of eternity . . . time given to Christ is never time lost, but is time rather gained, so that our relationships and indeed our whole life may become more profoundly human.

— *Dies Domini ("The Lord's Day")* #7

Consideration #29

Julian of Norwich had many powerful experiences of prayer. She also suffered much in her prayer. These experiences caused her to say, "The best prayer is to rest in the goodness of God, knowing that that goodness can reach right down to our lowest depths of need."

How can we rest in the goodness of God? To rest in the goodness of God is to surrender to stillness. To let go, to surrender, to abandon oneself.

TIME OUT! Rabbi Abraham Heschel, in his book Quest for God, *has this to say:*

We do not refuse to pray; we abstain from it.
We ring the hollow bell of selfishness rather than absorb

the stillness that surrounds the world, hovering over all the restlessness and fear of life — the secret stillness that precedes our birth and succeeds our death. Futile self-indulgence brings us out of tune with the gentle song of nature's waiting, of mankind's striving for salvation. Is not listening to the pulse of wonder worth silence and abstinence from self-assertion? Why do we not set apart an hour of living for devotion to God by surrendering to stillness? We dwell on the edge of mystery and ignore it, wasting our souls, risking our stake in God. We constantly pour our inner light away from Him, setting up the thick screen of self between Him and us, adding more shadows to the darkness that already hovers between Him and our wayward reason. Accepting surmises as dogmas, and prejudices as solutions, we ridicule the evidence of life for what is more than life. Our mind has ceased to be sensitive to wonder. Deprived of the power of devotion to what is more important than one individual fate, steeped in passionate anxiety, to survive, we loose sight of what fate is, of what living is. Rushing through the ecstasies of ambition, we only awake when plunged into dread or grief. In darkness, then, we grope for solace, for meaning, for prayer.

Consideration #30

What is contemplative prayer?

According to "Big T" (St. Teresa of Ávila), this "is nothing else than a close sharing between friends; it means taking time frequently to be alone with him who we know loves us" (CCC #2709).

Of course you've got to establish that friendship first!

Consideration #31

Adoration of Jesus in the Blessed Sacrament is an awesome school of prayer. Just to sit in the presence of Jesus can produce tremendous effects in our lives.

As Pope John Paul II said in his year 2000 Holy Thursday Letter to Priests: "There we will learn the secret of overcoming our solitude; receive the strength to bear all sufferings; the nourishment to make new beginnings after every discouragement; and the inner energy to bolster our decision to remain faithful."

Consideration #32

The Jesus Prayer — "Lord Jesus Christ, Son of God, have mercy on me a sinner" — is a powerful prayer.

Just to say the Holy Name of Jesus is a powerful prayer. To grow ever more in love with Jesus is a sure way to grow in prayer. This is what happened to St. Francis of Assisi. It can happen to you!

TIME OUT! Read this about the experience of St. Francis, from Thomas of Celano's First Life of *St. Francis:*

He was always occupied with Jesus. Jesus he bore in his heart, Jesus in his ears, Jesus in his eyes, Jesus in his hands, Jesus in the rest of his members. O how often, when he sat down to eat, hearing or speaking or thinking of Jesus, he forgot bodily food . . . indeed, many times, as he went along the way meditating and singing of Jesus, he would forget his journey and invite all the elements to praise Jesus.

Consideration #33

Mothers have a powerful and unique way of teachin their children. This is true even more so with our Heavenly Mother. She has a unique way of teachin and helpin us to pray.

St. Francis turned to the Blessed Mother with great love so she could help him love Jesus and live the Gospel, holdin nothin back of himself for himself but rather givin it all for Jesus. She can help us too!

TIME OUT! St. Bonaventure, in his Major Life of St. Francis, *says this:*

He prayed to her who had conceived the Word, full of grace and truth, imploring her with continual sighs to become his advocate. Through the merits of the mother of Mercy, he conceived and brought to birth the spirit and truth of the Gospel.

Rejoice always, pray without ceasing, give thanks in all circumstances; for this is the will of God in Christ Jesus for you.

1 Thessalonians 5:16-18

CHAPTER 7

Prayers: Now U Talkin!

1. Prayer for Help

Lord, take control!

2. Prayer for Serenity

(By Reinhold Niebuhr)

God, grant me the serenity
To accept the things I cannot change,
Courage to change the things I can,
And wisdom to know the difference.
Living one day at a time,
Enjoying one moment at a time,
Accepting hardship as a way to peace,
Taking, as Jesus did,
This sinful world as it is,
Not as I would have it,
Trusting that You will make all things right,
If I surrender to Your will,
So that I may be reasonably happy in this life,
And supremely happy with You forever in the next.
Amen.

3. Prayer of Abandonment

(By Bl. Charles de Foucauld)

Father, I abandon myself into Your hands;
Do with me what You will.
Whatever You may do
I thank You;
I am ready for all, I accept all.
Let only Your will be done in me
and in all Your creatures —
I wish no more than this, O Lord.
Into Your hands I commend my soul;
I offer it to You
with all the love of my heart,
for I love You, Lord,
and so need to give myself,
to surrender myself into Your hands,
without reserve,
and with boundless confidence,
for You are my Father.

4. The Universal Prayer

(Attributed to Pope Clement XI)

Lord, I believe in you: increase my faith.
I trust in you: strengthen my trust.
I love you: let me love you more and more.
I am sorry for my sins: deepen my sorrow.

I worship you as my first beginning,
I long for you as my last end,
I praise you as my constant helper,
And call on you as my loving protector.

Guide me by your wisdom,

Correct me with your justice,
Comfort me with your mercy,
Protect me with your power.

I offer you, Lord, my thoughts: to be fixed on you;
My words: to have you as their theme;
My actions: to reflect my love for you;
My sufferings: to be endured for your greater glory.

I want to do what you ask of me:
In the way you ask,
For as long as you ask,
Because you ask it.

Lord, enlighten my understanding,
Strengthen my will,
Purify my heart,
And make me holy.

Help me to repent of my past sins
And to resist temptation in the future.
Help me to rise above my human weaknesses
And to grow stronger as a Christian.

Let me love you, my Lord and my God,
And see myself as I really am:
A pilgrim in this world,
A Christian called to respect and love
All whose lives I touch,
Those in authority over me
Or those under my authority,
My friends and my enemies.

Help me to conquer anger with gentleness,
Greed by generosity,
Apathy by fervor.
Help me to forget myself

And reach out toward others.

Make me prudent in planning,
Courageous in taking risks.
Make me patient in suffering,
Unassuming in prosperity.

Keep me, Lord, attentive at prayer,
Temperate in food and drink,
Diligent in my work,
Firm in my good intentions.

Let my conscience be clear,
My conduct without fault,
My speech blameless,
My life well-ordered.

Put me on guard against my human weaknesses.
Let me cherish your love for me,
Keep your law,
And come at last to your salvation.

Teach me to realize that this world is passing,
That my true future is the happiness of heaven,
That life on earth is short,
And the life to come eternal.

Help me to prepare for death
With a proper fear of judgment,
But a greater trust in your goodness.
Lead me safely through death
To the endless joy of heaven.

Grant this through Christ our Lord. Amen.

5. Prayer of St. Thomas Aquinas Before Mass

Almighty and ever-living God,
I approach the sacrament of your only-begotten Son,
Our Lord Jesus Christ.
I come sick to the doctor of life,
Unclean to the fountain of mercy,
Blind to the radiance of eternal light,
And poor and needy to the Lord of heaven and earth.
Lord, in your great generosity,
Heal my sickness, wash away my defilement,
Enlighten my blindness, enrich my poverty,
And clothe my nakedness.
May I receive the bread of angels,
The King of kings and Lord of lords,
With humble reverence,
With the purity and faith,
The repentance and love, and the determined purpose
That will help to bring me to salvation.
May I receive the sacrament of the Lord's body and
     blood,
In its reality and power.
Kind God,
May I receive the body of your only begotten Son,
Our Lord Jesus Christ,
Born from the womb of the Virgin Mary,
And so be received into his mystical body
And numbered among his members.
Loving Father,
As on my earthly pilgrimage
I now receive your beloved Son
Under the veil of a sacrament,
May I one day see him face to face in glory,
Who lives and reigns with you forever. Amen.

6. Prayer of St. Thomas Aquinas After Mass

Lord, Father all-powerful and ever-living God,
I thank you,
For even though I am a sinner, your unprofitable servant,
Not because of my worth, but in the kindness of your
    mercy,
You have fed me with the precious body and blood of
    your Son,
Our Lord Jesus Christ.
I pray that this holy communion
May not bring me condemnation and punishment
But forgiveness and salvation.
May it be a helmet of faith
And a shield of good will.
May it purify me of evil ways
And put an end to my evil passions.
May it bring me charity and patience,
Humility and obedience,
And growth in the power to do good.
May it be my strong defense
Against all my enemies, visible and invisible,
And the perfect calming of all my evil impulses,
Bodily and spiritual.
May it unite me more closely to you,
The one true God
And lead me safely through death
To everlasting happiness with you.
And I pray that you will lead me, a sinner,
To the banquet where you,
With your Son and Holy Spirit,
Are true and perfect light,
Total fulfillment, everlasting joy,
Gladness without end,
And perfect happiness to your saints.
Grant this through Christ out Lord. Amen.

7. Prayer Not to be Disturbed

(*By St. Teresa of Ávila [*"Big T"*]*)

Let nothing disturb you.
Let nothing frighten you.
All things pass.
God never changes.
Patience attains all that it strives for.
He who has God finds he lacks nothing.
God alone suffices.

8. Prayer to End Abortion

(From *In the Zone — A Teen Guide to Prayer*)

Father, we beg your blessing for the Right to Life,
the unborn, the weak, the sick and the old;
all who are finding themselves being targets
of the vicious culture of death;
that our Lord Jesus bless and protect all who stand up
for the Christian dignity of persons.
That God enlighten those who are traveling
down death's highway
by their involvement, in any way,
with either the contemporary death culture,
selfism, relativism, or any of the new age errors
of our times, that God envelop our culture with
His Divine protection and help us both individually
and as a nation to true enlightenment,
conversion and repentance of ourselves
and our culture. Help us to turn from our
national sin of abortion, and return to, and
once again become a Christian nation,
on the narrow road, that is,
the path to becoming
a nation and culture, under God.
Amen.

9. Prayer to Your Guardian Angel

Angel of God,
My guardian dear,
To whom God's love
Commits me here.
Ever this day
Be at my side,
To light and guard,
To rule and guide.
Amen.

10. Prayer for Confession (An Act of Contrition)

O my God, I am sorry for my sins
with all my heart.
In choosing to do wrong
and failing to do good
I have sinned against You
Whom I should love
above all things.
I firmly resolve
with the help of Your grace
to sin no more and to
avoid the near occasion of sin.
Our Savior Jesus Christ
suffered and died for us.
In His Name, my God,
have mercy.
Amen.

11. Prayer of St. Ignatius of Loyola

Lord Jesus Christ, take all my freedom,
My memory, my understanding,
And my will.
All that I have and cherish
You have given me.
I surrender it all
To be guided by Your will.
Your grace and Your love
Are wealth enough for me.
Give me these, Lord Jesus,
And I ask for nothing more.

12. Prayer to St. Michael the Archangel

St. Michael the Archangel,
Defend us in battle.
Be our protection against the wickedness
And snares of the devil.
May God rebuke him, we humbly pray,
And do you, O Prince of the Heavenly Host,
By the power of God
Cast into hell Satan
And all the evil spirits
Who wander the world
Seeking the ruin of souls.
Amen.

13. Prayer for Self-mastery

(Based on Sirach 22:27-23:6)

Who will set a guard over my mouth,
And upon my lips an effective seal,
That I may not fail through them,
That my tongue may not destroy me?
["I tell you, on the day of judgement
you will have to render an account
for every careless word you utter" (Matthew 12:36).]
Lord, Father and master of my life,
Permit me not to fall by them!
Who will apply the lash to my thoughts,
To my mind the rod of discipline,
That my failings may not be spared,
Nor the sins of my heart overlooked;
Lest my failings increase,
And my sins be multiplied;
Lest I succumb to my foes,
And my enemies rejoice over me.
Lord, Father and God of my life,
Abandon me not into their control!
A brazen look allow me not;
Ward off passion from my heart,
Let not the lustful cravings of the flesh master me,
Surrender me not to shameless desires.

14. Prayer to the Holy Spirit

(By St. Augustine)

Breathe in me, Holy Spirit,
That all my thoughts may be holy.
Move in me, Holy Spirit,
That my work, too, may be holy.
Attract my heart, Holy Spirit,
That I may love only what is holy.
Strengthen me, Holy Spirit,
That I may defend all that is holy.
Protect me, Holy Spirit,
That I always may be holy.

15. Prayer for Your Family

Lord Jesus, I pray for my family.
Bless those who help me
and bless those who hurt me.
Bless those who are at home
and bless those who are away from home.
Bless those whom I find easy to love
and bless those whom I find
difficult/impossible to love.
Lord, bless all the members
of my family who have died.
Bless them with eternal rest and peace.
Lord, bless all the members of my family.

16. Prayer to Know and Do God's Will

Lord Jesus,
Doing the Father's will
was Your food.
You lived and died for it.
Help me to be open to know
and strengthened to do
the Father's will.
Help me to be
as committed to it
and as passionate about it
as You were.
It is only in
knowing and doing
the Father's will that
I will be happy
and at peace.
Holy Spirit,
Command me to do
Your holy will.

17. Prayer for When You're Confused

Lord Jesus, I'm really confused.
I really don't know why
and I don't know what to do
and I can't help the way I feel.
So I'm coming to You.
Lord Jesus, speak a Word
to scatter the darkness
in my mind and heart.
Burn away the clouds of uncertainty.
Shed a ray of Your Divine Light
With its healing rays to set me straight.
My mind, my heart, my body, my soul,

I give to You . . . take control.
Jesus, I trust in You.

18. Prayer of Thanksgiving

Lord, I could never thank You enough,
so I thank You as I can.
Please give me a grateful heart
so I can appreciate all You are
and all You do for me
and for everyone everywhere.
Things could always be better
and things could also be worse.
But I just want to thank You for right now.
Thank You for the faith to believe that
I can do all things through You
Who strengthens me.
Thanks for not giving me
any more than I can handle.
Sometimes You have
a very high opinion of me
and for this, too, I thank You.
Help me to see and know myself
as You see and know me.
To see and love others
as You see and love them.
To see and love me
as You see and love me.
Thank You, Lord.

19. Prayer of an Inner-city Youth

(By Celestino "Pyro" Santiago)

Yo Lord I hear You got plans
Get me out-a-here it's killin me
Tryin to do good in the hood
But the devil is grillin me.
Gime Ya strength God
Show me You feelin me.
I'm too young for this torment
I'm livin in misery.
Every day time goes by
Shots get popped gotta make legal money
Stay away from the cops
The block is hot
And I ain't walkin away in them locks.
I'm with You Lord
I'm givin You the utmost props.
Now-a-daz haters result in violence
I'm lookin for that good life
Livin in silence.
I wanna live in peace
No more wildin.
Kids walkin down streets
Huggin and smilin.
Don't gotta worry bout
Hearin them sirens
Gunz firin
Boys dyin before they men
The demon seeks revenge.
Catch me posted with the MC priest
We can beat the beast
I hear You got plans.

20. Prayer of St. Thérèse of Lisieux ('Little T')

(From *The Story of A Soul*)

Open the Book of life, Lord Jesus;
See all the deeds recorded by the saints!
All these I want to perform for You!
What can You say in the face of
all this foolishness of mine,
for surely I am the weakest soul on earth?
Yet just because I am so weak
You have been pleased to grant
my childish little desires,
and now You will grant the rest,
other desires far greater than the Universe.

21. Prayer Before You Watch TV or Go to a Movie

(From *In the Zone — A Teen Guide to Prayer*)

Jesus, I want to use my mind
only for what is good,
what is pure and holy.
In my mind are thoughts of you;
help me to not clutter my mind
with any impurity.
Give me the grace I need
to resist temptations to watch, or look, or listen
at any impure or violent thing
that would be a distraction
to my mind's thoughts
of you and higher things.
Protect me from any image or sound
that would lead me away from you.
In Jesus' name. Amen.

22. Prayer Before You Go on a Date

(From In the Zone — A Teen Guide to Prayer)

Lord Jesus, I ask you for your protection tonight,
for me and my date.
Put a hedge of your protection around us,
around the vehicle we will be traveling in,
and around all the others we will be with.
I plead your precious blood over both of us,
and pray that no evil influence of any kind
would be able to prevail over us.
Especially protect us
from any impurity,
with each other or even in our minds.

23. Prayer After You Go on a Date

(From In the Zone — A Teen Guide to Prayer)

Jesus, thank you for your protection tonight.
Thank you for caring for us,
and for keeping us safe.
I commend my date to you tonight
and ask that your special blessing
would be upon their life
and of their entire family.
In Jesus' name. Amen.

24. Prayer for Your Friends

(From *In the Zone — A Teen Guide to Prayer*)

Jesus, thank you for my friends.
I ask for your blessing
on my friends today.
Show them your great love for them,
and if any are struggling or lonely,
hurting or broken in any way,
care for their needs
and comfort them as only you can.
Give me the graces I need to be a good friend —
open and trusting, caring and giving.
Help me to see my friends
with your eyes,
so I can see
when they are hurting on the inside
even though they don't show it
on the outside.
And most of all,
give me your heart
and your love for my friends,
so that I could love them as you do.
In Jesus' name. Amen.

25. Prayer for the Poor in the World

(From *In the Zone — A Teen Guide to Prayer*)

Father, you provide for the needs of the whole world.
There are millions who go hungry every day,
with not enough food to eat,
not enough clothes to wear,
and no home to live in.
Feed their bodies
and feed their souls.
Help me turn the sin in my life
that makes me selfish
and causes me to overlook
the needs of those around me every day.
Help me to share the blessings of my life
with others who are less fortunate than me.

Lord, how you love the poor.
You were poor yourself
and lived a life of simplicity.
You could have been rich
with all the material possessions
the world had to offer,
yet you chose to live simply,
but to be rich in your soul.
I pray for the poor of the world.
I pray that they would find richness in their soul,
because of their faith in you.
And I pray that you would not abandon them,
but would provide for their needs.
Give them the food they need to eat,
the clothes they need to wear
and a shelter for them to live.
Work in the hearts of those who have all that they need
and convict them of the need to share

the gifts they have received with
those less fortunate than them.

26. Prayer Before the Crucifix

(By St. Francis of Assisi)

Most high,
Glorious God,
Enlighten the darkness of my heart
And give me, Lord,
A correct faith,
A certain hope,
A perfect charity,
Sense and knowledge,
So that I may carry out Your holy and true command.

27. Prayer for Guidance

(By St. Francis of Assisi)

All-highest,
Glorious God,
Cast Your light
Into the darkness of my heart.
Give me a right faith,
A firm hope
And a perfect charity
With wisdom and insight,
O Lord,
So that I may
Do what is truly Your will.

28. Prayer for Self-confidence

(From *In the Zone — A Teen Guide to Prayer*)

Father, help me to do my best.
Help me to be confident,
not just in my own skills,
but in the fact that
you are always with me.
Inspire confidence in me
because of your presence
in my life.
Help me to show goodness
and kindness
to others, and to always
be aware of the needs
of those around me.

29. Prayer for the Gifts of the Holy Spirit

(By *St. Alphonsus Liguori*)

Holy Spirit, divine Consoler,
I adore You as my true God,
With God the Father and God the Son.
I adore You and unite myself
To the adoration You receive
From the angels and saints.
I give You my heart and
I offer my ardent thanksgiving
For all the grace
Which You never cease to bestow on me.

O Giver of all supernatural gifts,
Who filled the soul of the Blessed Virgin Mary,
Mother of God,

With such immense favors,
I beg You to visit me
With Your grace and Your love
And to grant me the gift
Of holy *fear*,
So that it may act on me as a check
To prevent me from falling back
Into my past sins,
For which I beg pardon.

Grant me the gift of *piety*,
So that I may serve You
For the future with increased fervor,
Follow with more promptness
Your holy inspirations
And observe Your divine precepts
With greater fidelity.

Grant me the gift of *knowledge*,
So that I may know the things of God and,
Enlightened by Your holy teaching,
May walk, without deviation,
In the path of eternal salvation.

Grant me the gift of *fortitude*,
So that I may overcome courageously
All the assaults of the devil,
And all the dangers of this world
Which threaten the
Salvation of my soul.

Grant me the gift of *counsel*,
So that I may choose
What is more conducive
To my spiritual advancement
And may discover the wiles and snares
Of the tempter.

Grant me the gift of *understanding*,
So that I may apprehend the divine mysteries
And by contemplation of heavenly things
Detach my thoughts and affections
From the vain things of this miserable world.

Grant me the gift of *wisdom*,
So that I may rightly direct all my actions,
Referring them to God
As my last end;
So that, having loved Him
And served Him
In this life,
I may have the happiness
Of possessing Him
Eternally in the next.
Amen.

30. Prayer to Mother Mary

("Salutations" by St. Francis of Assisi)

Hail, O Lady,
Holy Queen,
Mary, holy Mother of God:
You are the virgin made church
And the one chosen by the most holy
Father in heaven
Whom He consecrated
With His most holy beloved Son
And with the Holy Spirit the Paraclete,
In whom there was and is
All the fullness of grace
And every good.
Hail, His Palace!
Hail, His Tabernacle!
Hail, His Home!

Hail, His Robe!
Hail, His Servant!
Hail, His Mother!
And, [hail] all you holy virtues
Which through the grace and light of the Holy Spirit
Are poured into the hearts of the faithful
So that from their faithless state
You may make them faithful to God.

31. The Memorare

Remember, O most gracious Virgin Mary,
That never was it known
That anyone who fled to your protection,
Implored your help,
Or sought your intercession,
Was left unaided.
Inspired by this confidence,
I fly unto you,
O Virgin of virgins, my Mother.
To you I come;
Before you I stand
Sinful and sorrowful.
O Mother of the Word Incarnate,
Despise not my petitions,
But in your mercy
Hear and answer me.
Amen.

32. Prayer for Priests

Lord Jesus, hear our prayer
for the spiritual renewal of priests.
Stir up Your Holy Spirit within them.
Give them enthusiasm for the Gospel,
courage in leadership,
humility in service,
and zeal for the salvation of all people.
Let Your presence be in their hearts,
Your holiness in their souls,
Your joy in their spirits.
Inspire, guide, and bless their priestly service
and keep them united to You
With a never-ending love.
We pray to You, O Lord,
through Mary the Mother of all priests,
for Your priests and for ours.
Amen.

33. My Prayer 4 U

(Ephesians 3:14-21)

For this reason
I bow my knees before the Father,
from whom every family
in heaven and on earth takes its name.
I pray that, according to the riches of his glory,
he may grant that you may be strengthened
in your inner being with power through his Spirit,
and that Christ may dwell in your hearts through faith,
as you are being rooted and grounded in love.
I pray that you may have the power to comprehend,
    with all the saints,
what is the breadth and length and height and depth,
and to know the love of Christ that surpasses
    knowledge,
so that you may be filled with all the fullness of God.
Now to him who by the power at work within us is able
    to accomplish abundantly
far more than all we can ask or imagine,
to him be glory in the church and in Christ Jesus to all
    generations,
forever and ever. Amen.

APPENDIX

Examination of Conscience

I hope this little examination of conscience helps you to do just that — examine your conscience.

Hopefully, you will go to confession at least once a month and make a really good, honest, gut-spillin, soul-cleansin confession. This will give you access to the love and mercy of Jesus, which will help you to begin the long journey of conquerin your fears. You will deepen and strengthen your interior life.

Take it one day, one step at a time — just keep walkin on the path followin Jesus! Then you will be ready, willin, and able to follow the lead of JP:

It is time to put aside all fear and pursue daring apostolic goals. *Duc in altum!* ["Put out into the deep!"] (Lk 5:4): Christ's invitation spurs us to put out into the deep and to nourish ambitious dreams of personal holiness and apostolic fruitfulness. The apostolate always overflows from one's interior life. Certainly, it is also action, but action sustained by love. And the source of love always lies in a person's deepest dimension, where the voice of Christ is heard inviting us to put out into the deep with him. May each one of you welcome this invitation of Christ and respond to it with fresh generosity every day.
(*L'Osservatore Romano*, March 28, 2001, p. 6)

I pray that as you examine your conscience and make great confessions, you will have fresh generosity every day to follow Jesus and do the will of the heavenly Father in your life:

1. Relationships — I AM THE LORD YOUR GOD: YOU SHALL NOT HAVE STRANGE GODS BEFORE ME.

Do I put any one or anything before God? Family, friends, boyfriend, girlfriend, career, sports, my looks, my health, my future, studies, money, music, the opinion that others have of me? Bein accepted by the crowd? Do I make a strange god out of drugs, alcohol, or sex? TV, video games, the computer, and e-mail? The telephone? What areas of my life are lackin in trustin God? Do I doubt God's power to love and forgive me? Do I pray every day — read the Bible, pray the Rosary, make visits to the Blessed Sacrament? Do I try to keep God first in my life?

2. Mouth — YOU SHALL NOT TAKE THE NAME OF THE LORD YOUR GOD IN VAIN.

Wasss up with my mouth? Do I say "Oh God!" and not finish the sentence? (I could finish the sentence, like, "Oh God, please help me be more patient.") Do I curse and use foul language? Have I offended God's name by disrespectin the name and reputation of some of His children? Do I talk one way in front one group of people and another way with another group of people? Do I speak highly of God to my family and friends, or am I embarrassed and afraid to talk about Him?

3. Worship — REMEMBER TO KEEP HOLY THE LORD'S DAY.

Do I go to church every Sunday? (*Every* Sunday, not "most Sundays." "Almost" don't pay da rent! You got to go to Mass every Sunday. It's a serious sin and needs to be confessed). Do I make Sunday, the Lord's Day, a special day? Have I missed Mass on any holy days of obligation? Do I dress properly and in a way that shows the Lord's Day is special when I go to church? Do I do anything special on the Lord's Day to make it holy — any works of charity, special readin or prayin — or do I treat the Lord's Day as any other day? Do I prepare for the Lord's Day with monthly confession? Do I look at the readings before Sunday Mass? How have I failed to make every day holy?

4. Parents — HONOR YOUR FATHER AND YOUR MOTHER.

Do I honor and respect my parents, even if I don't get along with them? Even if I don't like them, do I still respect and honor them — even if it's "only" for the gift of life that God gave to me through them? How about the other members of my family, my community, my parish, and my friends? If my parents are divorced, have I sinned due to uncontrollable anger and frustration? Have I been so attached to my parents that I put them before God — even if I don't know who my mother or father is?

5. Anger — YOU SHALL NOT KILL.

Does anger have a grip on me? Do I have violent thoughts toward others or myself? Do I watch violent movies and play violent video/computer games? Have I ever physically hurt or attempted to hurt someone? Have I ever thought of killin anybody? Have I ever thought about or attempted to take my own life? Did I ever have an abortion or help someone else have an abortion? Do I speak up for life and God's plan, or do I keep a deadly, cowardly silence in the presence of certain people? Do I have any hate in my heart? Have I corrected someone without kindness and compassion? Have I done violence to my body by using drugs, alcohol, eating too much food or the wrong food, reckless driving, or taking foolish and dangerous risks? Have I caused disruption in the peace of others because of my bad behavior and bad attitude?

6. Sex — YOU SHALL NOT COMMIT ADULTERY.

Have I entertained impure thoughts without prayin for help? Have I acted on those thoughts with myself (that is, masturbation)? Am I sexually active in any kind of way? Do I engage in premarital sex — fornication? Do I show reverence and respect for the gift of my body and for the sacredness of the bodies of others as temples of the Holy Spirit? Do I look at pornography (magazines, videos, Internet, trash novels, audio-pornography on some really bad music CDs)? Do I engage in lustful looks and thoughts? Do I engage in passionate kisses and sinful touchin of private parts? Do I love myself in a selfish way? Have I been lazy with my prayers and in reading the Bible? Do I have respect for the same and the opposite sex? Have I been immodest in my dress and choice of entertainment? Have I been respectful to people who struggle with homosexual feelings and are tryin to live a chaste life?

7. Stealin — YOU SHALL NOT STEAL.

Have I taken anything that is not mine? Have I stolen from my parents or my brothers and sisters? Have I cheated at school? Have I stolen anything from work, includin time? Am I honest with my responsibilities? Am I generous in sharing with others — my time, talents, and possessions? Do I return what I borrow, and is it returned in good condition? Have I stolen time from God with spiritual laziness? Do I realize that all I have is a gift from God? Am I grateful?

8. Lyin — YOU SHALL NOT BEAR FALSE WITNESS AGAINST YOUR NEIGHBOR.

Do I lie? If so, how often? Do I think that "small" lies are OK? Do I confess all the lies — big and small? Do I lie out of convenience? Am I afraid of the truth? Do I distort the truth to put others down? Do I distort the truth to make me look good? Do I judge others, either in my mind or in my conversations about them? Do I assume the worst or the best about others? Do I give others the benefit of the doubt? Do I gossip and talk bad about others behind their back? Are there any ways I have been deceitful? Have I revealed any secrets that people have entrusted to me? Have I betrayed the confidence of a friend?

9. Envy — YOU SHALL NOT COVET YOUR NEIGHBOR'S WIFE.

Am I jealous of another person's gifts and talents? Am I jealous of other people's relationships? Am I envious of someone else's body, looks, gifts, talents, or personality? Do I appreciate and take care of my body? Am I grateful for the person God made me? Do I hate my body and myself? Do I use the gifts and talents God gave me? Do I compliment people for their gifts and talents, and therefore give glory to God by buildin them up? Do I let my imagination run wild in a sinful way? Do I take the call to holiness seriously? Do I share myself and my gifts with others generously? Am I kind to strangers and to those who seem to be alone?

10.Greed — YOU SHALL NOT COVET YOUR NEIGHBOR'S GOODS.

Do I dwell on material possessions? Do I value things over people? Is my heart greedy? Am I jealous of the material possessions other people have? Am I envious of what others have? Am I content with what I have? Am I bitter because I might not have all the things I want? How am I selfish with regard to material possessions? Do I share what I have generously and willingly, or do I complain? Do I seek consolation in material possessions, in food, or in any person or thing before God? Do I appreciate what others have, and do I thank God for the ways He has blessed others?

About the Author

Father Stan Fortuna is a member of the Franciscan Friars of the Renewal. He uses the Lord's gift of music in his preaching as well as in his writing. Father Stan spends two-thirds of his time crossing the globe, preaching the Gospel of Jesus. The rest of his time is spent with his brothers, serving the poor in the South Bronx. He established Francesco Productions (www.francescoproductions.com), a nonprofit record company that contributes to the new evangelization and assists the Franciscan community's work with the poor.

Father Stan is also the author of *U Got 2 Pray.*

Notes

Notes

Notes

Notes

Notes

Notes

Notes

Notes

Notes

Our Sunday Visitor . . .
Your Source for Discovering
the Riches of the Catholic Faith

Our Sunday Visitor has an extensive line of materials for young children, teens, and adults. Our books, Bibles, booklets, CD-ROMs, audios, and videos are available in bookstores worldwide.

To receive a FREE full-line catalog or for more information, call **Our Sunday Visitor** at **1-800-348-2440**. Or write, **Our Sunday Visitor** / 200 Noll Plaza / Huntington, IN 46750.

- -

Please send me: ___A catalog
Please send me materials on:
___Apologetics and catechetics   ___Reference works
___Prayer books   ___Heritage and the saints
___The family   ___The parish
Name_____
Address_____Apt._____
City_____State_____Zip_____
Telephone (   ) _____

A19BBABP

- -

Please send a friend: ___A catalog
Please send a friend materials on:
____Apologetics and catechetics   ____Reference works
____Prayer books   ____Heritage and the saints
____The family   ____The parish
Name_____
Address_____Apt._____
City_____State_____Zip_____
Telephone (   ) _____

A19BBABP

- -

Our Sunday Visitor
200 Noll Plaza
Huntington, IN 46750
Toll free: **1-800-348-2440**
E-mail: osvbooks@osv.com
Website: www.osv.com